Modern Writers

The 'Modern Writers' series

The following are titles in this new series of short guides to contemporary international writers:

John Crick

Robert Lowell

BARNES & NOBLE
BOOKS
10 East 53d St., New York 10022
(a division of Harper & Row Publishers, Inc.)

For my mother,
and in memory of my father

Published in the USA 1974 by
Harper & Row, Publishers, Inc.
Barnes & Noble Import Division

Oliver & Boyd

Croythorn House
23 Ravelston Terrace
Edinburgh EH4 3TJ
A Division of Longman Group Ltd

© 1974 John Crick

ISBN 06 491316-3

Printed in Great Britain by
T. & A. Constable Ltd, Edinburgh

Contents

Contents

Acknowledgements

For permission to quote from the following works, all copyright by Robert Lowell, acknowledgements are due to Faber & Faber Ltd. and Farrar, Straus and Giroux, Inc.—*Imitations* © 1958, 1959, 1960, 1961—*Notebook* © 1967, 1968, 1969, 1970—*For the Union Dead* © 1956, 1960, 1961, 1962, 1963, 1964—*Near the Ocean* © 1963, 1965, 1966, 1967—*Life Studies* © 1956, 1959—*Phaedra* © 1960, 1961; and for *Poems* © 1950, *Lord Weary's Castle and The Mills of the Kavanaughs* © 1961, 1968 to Faber & Faber Ltd. and Harcourt Brace Jovanovich Inc.

Note

Abbreviations by which the works of Robert Lowell and others are quoted in footnotes:

F.U.D.	*For the Union Dead*
I.	*Imitations*
L.S.	*Life Studies*
L.U.	*Land of Unlikeness*
M.K.	*The Mills of the Kavanaughs*
N.	*Notebook*
N.O.	*Near the Ocean*
O.G.	*The Old Glory*
P.	*Poems 1938–1949*
P.B.	*Prometheus Bound*
PH.	*Phaedra*
P.R.	The *Paris Review* interview with Frederick Seidel, as reprinted in *Modern Poets on Modern Poetry*, ed. James Scully
Alvarez	'A Talk with Robert Lowell', in *Encounter*, February 1965
London and Boyers	*Robert Lowell: A Portrait of the Artist in his Time*, ed. Michael London and Robert Boyers
Naipaul	V. S. Naipaul conversation with Lowell, in *The Listener*, 4 September 1969
Ostroff	*The Contemporary Poet as Artist and Critic*, ed. Anthony Ostroff
Parkinson	*Robert Lowell: A Collection of Critical Essays*, ed. T. Parkinson
Price	*Critics on Robert Lowell*, ed. Jonathan Price
Staples	Hugh B. Staples, *Robert Lowell: The First Twenty Years*

1   Exile and Return

Here is an extract from Robert Lowell's short prose autobiography, '91 Revere Street':[1]

> Undoubtedly Major Mordecai had lived in a more ritualistic, gaudy, and animal world than twentieth-century Boston. There was something undecided, Mediterranean, versatile, almost double-faced about his bearing which suggested that, even to his contemporaries, he must have seemed gratuitously both *ci-devant* and *parvenu*. He was a dark man, a German Jew—no downright Yankee, but maybe such a fellow as Napoleon's mad, pomaded son-of-an-innkeeper-general, Junot, Duc D'Abrantes; a man like mad George III's pomaded, disreputable son, 'Prinny', the Prince Regent. Or he was one of those Moorish-looking dons painted by his contemporary, Goya—some leader of Spanish guerillas against Bonaparte's occupation, who fled to South America. Our Major's suffering almond eye rested on his luxurious dawn-coloured fingers ruffling an off-white glove.[2]

The passage is an attempt by the adult Lowell to convey the impression made on his younger self by a figure in a family portrait. A great-great-grandfather on the father's side, Major Mordecai Myers comes across as a quixotically-attractive figure with an air of decidedly unmilitary non-conformity. Each detail is dwelt on fondly and nostalgically by the writer, who has confessed that he got more than an ordinary boy's pleasure out of toy soldiers and memorising the names of French generals, and

1. *L.S.*, pp. 19–59.
2. *L.S.*, pp. 19–20.

who has celebrated military qualities in an often idiosyncratic way, even to describing Nathaniel Hawthorne as a Civil War officer with a 'General Custer scalp'.[3] But the references to madness and to the 'suffering almond eye' ruffle the surface of the slightly rococo prose style and suggest that the major is more to his recorder than a warmly-remembered individualist; and the characterisation of Boston hints at how much New England and its traditions depended upon a conjunction of capitalist, religious and racial orthodoxies—to which a real-life Major Myers would seem implicitly a threat. Alas, this nineteenth-century exotic never existed—outside his portrait and his young admirer's fantasies; the historical major, we are told a few lines later, was as tamely honourable and unoutrageous as Boston ever knew.

'91 Revere Street' is a record of several such disenchantments; but behind them all is a basic quarrel with a city for permitting them to happen. Boston wears many faces in Robert Lowell's poetry—a Baudelairean nightmare, a City of Dreadful Night, the *urbs* of Juvenal and Horace are just a few; but always, it represents some lost ideal. Historically, the city has a special claim to uniqueness, for as Malcolm Bradbury has indicated, the Boston of 1830–60 was the only American milieu ever successfully to put into practice 'the belief that [a] culture could be transformed through the witness of the writer and intellectual'.[4] In a conversation with the novelist V. S. Naipaul, Lowell himself expatiated on this theme: '. . . somehow by about 1830 the other cities didn't exist for a while—and I mean by "Boston", not only Boston itself, but Cambridge and Concord and New England in general, and people like James and Melville, who came from other places to New England. So it was one of the great moments of the 19th century.'[5] Socially, Boston represented that aristocratic strain in democratic America which speaks, however crudely, through Captain Delano in Lowell's adaptation of Melville's 'Benito Cereno': 'We need inferiors, Perkins, / more manners, more docility, no one has an inferior mind in America'.[6]

3. *F.U.D.*, p. 39.
4. *The Social Context of Modern English Literature*, Oxford (Basil Blackwell) 1971, p. 39.
5. *Naipaul*, p. 302.
6. *O.G.*, p. 168.

But when Lowell arrived on the scene, all that was left was the mere 'shell of [a] stark culture';[7] and now, as Elizabeth Hardwick once put it, in contemporary Boston, 'The old jokes embarrass, the anecdotes are so many thrice-squeezed lemons, and no new fruit hangs on the boughs.'[8] For Lowell, the city's decline as cultural ideal has always related to a vision of New England as failed metaphysical promise—

> Child, the Mayflower rots
> In your poor bred-out stock
>
> ('The Boston Nativity')

—but in the 1920's and 1930's of his youth, the failure seemed to hinge more narrowly on personal inadequacies, the effects of the Depression, and of racial and class changes in a fashionable part of Boston, the Beacon Hill district. Symbolically, it is the story of the city's two famous parks—the once-exclusive Public Garden, and the Common—the story of how the values and inhabitants of the latter increasingly encroach on the former:

> . . . the poor dead cannot see Easter crowds
> On Boston Common or the Beacon Hill
> Where strangers hold the golden Statehouse dome
> For good and always.
>
> ('At the Indian Killer's Grave')

One of the more moving moments in '91 Revere Street' is the young Lowell's expulsion from the Public Garden for some minor, childish misdemeanour; so another version of a New World Eden ends.

Many people who have read Wallace Stevens, Robert Frost and William Carlos Williams for years would be hard put to it to recount more than a handful of facts about any of these poets' lives. Lowell's public biography is almost embarrassingly rich in detail. Born in 1917, he comes of a family which, on both the father's and the mother's (Winslow) sides, has contributed a great

7. *P.*, p. 31.
8. 'Boston', in *Encounter*, November 1959, p. 41.

3

deal to the political, military and cultural history of New England. America's and his family's histories have combined to give him a high sense of his calling as a poet, qualified by that feeling of the dubious privilege of exalted birth which makes his Prometheus say to the daughters of Ocean: 'You can thank your Father for your lowly birth. I was born higher and had less chance.'[9] Much returned to in his poetry, these ancestors include a 'Mayflower' pilgrim, a governor of Plymouth Colony, a general in the Revolutionary Wars, a president of Harvard, and an ambassador to England. This last was the once highly-esteemed James Russell Lowell, a Boston Brahmin and apostle of the more complacent virtues of the Boston-Cambridge cultural axis. Very much the public poet, his works include a long poem about Prometheus, which anticipates one of his great-great-nephew's symbolic roles, and such commemorative poems as: 'Ode read at the One Hundredth Anniversary of the Fight at Concord Bridge', 'Ode for the Fourth of July, 1876' and the 'Ode recited at the Harvard Commemoration, 1865', which contains these un-memorable lines:

> We sit here in the Promised Land
> That flows with Freedom's honey and milk.[10]

Though conspicuously ignored in the poetry of his descendant, he makes a brief appearance in an image of New England's cultural senility:

> Look at the faces—
> Longfellow, Lowell, Holmes and Whittier!
> Study the grizzled silver of their beards.
>
> ('Hawthorne')

In his own perverse way, however, he set an enviable standard, for the Boston insularity went with assurances of status and audience that made it possible for him to write, in the Harvard ode, a convincing public poem about America's national identity, the Civil War, and heroism.

9. *P.B.*, p. 53.
10. *Poems of James Russell Lowell*, London (O.U.P.) 1912, p. 487.

The other famous poet of the Lowell family was the eccentric black sheep described in '91 Revere Street', Amy Lowell. Very much a rebel against the Victorian stodginess of James Russell Lowell, a miniaturist and enthusiast for Chinese and Japanese poetry, she produced 'A Critical Fable', which is in part an ironic and often witty side-swipe at the older poet's 'A Fable for Critics':

> No one likes to be bound
> In a sort of perpetual family pound
> Tied by *esprit de corps* to the wheels of the dead[11]

—it is a feeling Robert Lowell must have often shared! Her 'escape' to London in 1913, where she became an enthusiastic publisher of Imagist anthologies, Eliot's 'demon saleswoman',[12] and organiser of the Imagist movement into a 'democratic beer-garden'[13] which Lawrence and Pound called 'Amygism', anticipates Lowell's flight from Harvard some twenty-five years later. Though it was largely because of her dubious reputation that Robert Lowell's father regarded the trade of writer as a disreputable one, for a would-be innovator and rebel ('like Mae West she seemed to provoke indecorum in others'[14]), she was curiously timid in some respects, her enthusiasm for the comparatively safely-rebellious Imagism contrasting with her unsympathetic attitude to Pound and Eliot; she found 'The Waste Land' 'immensely interesting as a state of mind', but not poetry.[15] Lowell has shown a warm affection for her spinsterish refusal to conform, even if little influence from her is apparent, except perhaps that the precision, economy and stress on the object of his later poetry reflect general Imagist aims.

Lowell's early life is the old story of social position without the means to live up to it; 'Cut down, we flourish', the family

11. *The Complete Poetical Works of Amy Lowell*, Boston (Houghton, Mifflin) 1955, p. 409.

12. Quoted in Louise Bogan, *Achievement in American Poetry, 1900–1950*, Chicago (Regnery) 1951, p. 53.

13. *The Letters of Ezra Pound, 1907–1941*, ed. D. D. Paige, London (Faber) 1951, p. 48.

14. *L.S.*, p. 50.

15. Amy Lowell, letter to Richard Aldington, 4 April 1923.

motto of the Winslows and of the Kavanaughs of a Lowell poem, has a pointedly ironic ring about it in the light of Lowell's parents. Lowell's father emerges from his son's account of his own Beacon Hill childhood as a pathetically inept, but not unlovable, ex-naval officer turned unsuccessful businessman, a man who had lost 'all freedom to explode';[16] the mother is a pushing, self-pitying snob who read books of psychiatry, discussed her husband's failings in front of others and expatiated on the decline of the family fortunes to her only child. She is trapped for ever in the 'superior' vagaries of her speech as recorded by her son:

'Your inebriated sailors have littered my doorstep with the dregs of Scollay Square'
'I have always believed carving to be *the* gentlemanly talent'
'Mamá always said that the *old* Hungarians *did* have taste'
'A really great person knows how to be courteous to his superiors'[17]

—the dominant women in Lowell's poetry seem monster-Clytemnestra-projections of this woman. For an alternative to the frustrated, alienated lives of these two, there was in the Revere Street circle the bluff confidence of an over-ripe America in Commander Billy Harkness, and an older, firmer-rooted individualism in the commercial pioneerings of Grandfather Winslow. Outside the home, there were the jockeyings for status and the minor gaffes of the Public Garden mini-world, and the harrowing experience of being a boy in a girls' school. Not surprisingly, the main impression left by '91 Revere Street' is of a child's searing loneliness. If Lowell seems to make too much of his portrait of Major Mordecai Myers in the early pages, it is probably a token of his respect for the Jewish quality of survival —the one quality his life has shown consistently—and a nostalgic regret for the lack in his own family of those family pieties which Jewish life traditionally fosters. '91 Revere Street' ends with the moving line: 'I know why young Bob is an only child';

16. *L.S.*, p. 38.
17. *L.S.*, respectively, pp. 34, 45, 51, 59.

a great deal of the rebellious behaviour of Lowell's early life suggests nothing so much as search for surrogate fathers and mothers—in Grandfather Winslow, poets of an older generation, and Harriet Winslow, his much-celebrated older cousin.

The shadow of rebellion has always haunted his poetry:

> Rebellion, sick with wrongs,
> now like a sea-beast, lifts its slimey prongs,
> its muck, its jelly.[18]

In an early poem, simply called 'Rebellion'[19] and about an incident in adolescence, the carefully-pointed details of the poem encourage the reader to see the rebellion in a larger context of New England and its past; Lowell's treatment of rebellion in his poetry has always had this capacity to widen out in this way. Very early, he saw his life as adding to that mixture of individualism and conformity peculiar to New England's writers: the Puritans, with their heroic, tragic vision; a later representative of the Puritan tradition in Jonathan Edwards, whose anguished sense of lost religious opportunities was muted in old age by a moving humanitarianism; the sense of man's overweening pride and of the omnipresence of evil in Hawthorne and Melville; the implicit denial of the existence of evil in the too benign, unheroic and romantic world-view of Emerson and Thoreau, from which both the supernatural and the physical is in retreat:

> Concord, where Thoreau
> And Emerson fleeced Heaven of Christ's robe.[20]

If by the latter years of the nineteenth century, New England's literary traditions had taken the twin roads of a tame Anglophilia and provinciality, there was still enough of the original sap to produce two late fruit in Eliot (Lowell has always considered him a New England poet) with his orientation towards Europe, and in Frost, with his native, older sensibility.

18. *PH.*, p. 39.
19. *P.*, p. 39.
20. From an early version of Lowell's 'Concord', in *Partisan Review*, X, July–August 1943, p. 316.

Significantly for Lowell, however, their initial impetus as poets came from a rejection of the city, even if a much more unambiguous, and in some ways, more radical rejection than the one that inspired his own earliest poetry.

Inevitably, Lowell entered Harvard, but after two years there during which he apparently wrote free verse, blank verse and poems in the manner of William Carlos Williams, he set out to seek his poetic fortunes (with the grudging blessing of his parents) at Kenyon College, Ohio, where he graduated in 1940. Lowell has often pointed out that the United States is a country evolved from a series of deliberate choices: the Constitution, the Declaration of Independence, for example. In one sense an existential plunge, in another, one of a number of psychic parricides in Lowell's life, his decision to go to Kenyon was at the simplest level a way of avoiding the fates that Ford Madox Ford, whom Lowell met at the time, predicted as the likely ones for a poet of the Boston Lowell family—a 'butterfly existence', the presidency of Harvard, or an ambassadorship to England.[21] But it was also in line with a main tendency of the modernist movement in literature: feelings of dispossession and a deep uncertainty about cultural standards, alongside a sense of the force of traditional values, and an urge for fulfilling an historical mission. Tradition, as Eliot puts it, 'cannot be inherited, and if you want it, you must obtain it by great labour'.[22]

At the time, Kenyon College was acquiring a reputation. Through John Crowe Ransom, under whom he studied at Kenyon, and Allen Tate whom he visited in Tennessee, Lowell was introduced to a group of Southern writers who had in various ways rejected what they conceived to be the North's misguided political, economic and cultural values. In social terms, the 'Fugitives' rejected the provincialism of the Old South in favour of a concern with Time, History and Myth, and in the pursuance of a life classical-minded, of a highly-wrought sophistication and decorum, and 'ritualistic, gaudy, and animal' in Major Myers' way. Their view of American decline as emanating from the city struck a responsive chord in Lowell's view of Boston; their

21. 'William Carlos Williams', in *Hudson Review*, XIV, 1961–62, p. 530.
22. 'Tradition and the Individual Talent', in *Selected Essays*, London (Faber) 1932, p. 14.

classicism encouraged a marked feature of his early work; and the glorification of the soldier-hero in the work of some members of the 'Southern Renaissance' was shared by a poet whose own poetry has military protagonists who often seem like doomed Confederate heroes. As with Lowell himself, the group's original position had been one of exile-within-society: in a poem in the first issue of the group's magazine, *The Fugitive*, Ransom referred to himself as 'an alien, miserably at feud / With those my generation'. At the time of *The Fugitive* (1922–25) the movement was associated with certain conservative, even reactionary policies, but by the late 'thirties, the political impulse had largely given way to a critical and academic one; Ransom founded the *Kenyon Review* in 1939 as a literary, not a political journal and the appearance of two poems[23] by Lowell in its first number (his first published work apart from poems in undergraduate magazines) was, therefore, not a commitment to a particular political viewpoint. Lowell's 'discovery' of the South was probably as significant for him as Eliot's of Europe and of the Metaphysicals, and as Pound's of Provençal culture and the East. One can say that he learned from the writers of the 'Southern Renaissance' how to be a traditional writer with regional roots, without the debilitating narrowness that often accompanies the type. In immediate terms it offered an alternative to both the political inspiration of much current poetry, and to the continuing force in American poetry of both Emily Dickinson's 'divine insanity' and Whitman's 'barbaric yawp', in a poetic orthodoxy with the stress on disciplined energies. As, in his own words, a 'second generation' fugitive, Lowell sees the 'Southern Renaissance' as marking a return to formality after the first stage of the modernist revolution in poetry with Eliot and Pound.[24]

Since those early years, Lowell has qualified his admiration for the movement, and seen implicit in it an 'inarticulate and immoral' attitude to the present.[25] In a witty prose recollection

23. 'The Cities' Summer Death' and 'The Dandelion Girls', in *Kenyon Review*, I, Winter 1939, pp. 32–3, with the laconic note: 'R. T. S. Lowell, of Boston, is a student of Kenyon College'.

24. Interview with A. Alvarez, 'Robert Lowell in Conversation', in *The Review*, 8, August 1963, pp. 38–9.

25. *Alvarez*, p. 43.

of the period, 'Visiting the Tates', he treats his own involvement with considerable irony at his own expense.[26] He refers to himself as a young man with 'Miltonic, vaguely piratical ambitions' crashing 'the civilisation of the South', and discovering himself as 'part of a legend. I was Northern, disembodied, a Platonist, a puritan, an abolitionist.' He began to despise 'the rootless appetites of middle-class meliorism'. The phrases he uses to describe the Tates—'Stately yet bohemian, leisurely yet dedicated'—suggest he found in them a cultural equivalent of the portrait Major Myers, and the terms he applies to Tate's poems—'a killing eloquence', 'the formal resonance of desperation'—could more than adequately relate to many of his own. One ambition the Kenyon experience might have fostered in a less resilient mind than Lowell's is that of becoming an Arnold or Vergil to modern America; if his career has done no more than glance at this possibility, it might be in some measure owing to the critical circles he moved in at this time, with their particular kinds of stringency. At Kenyon, he met Randall Jarrell, whom he has called both 'the most heartbreaking English poet . . . of his generation'[27] and its finest critic,[28] and in 1942–43, when he was teaching at Louisiana State University, Cleanth Brooks and Robert Penn Warren, who were then editing the *Southern Review*, and producing jointly a series of influential critical textbooks. Lowell has testified to his excitement about the critical scene at this period, with its suggestion of the possibility of a creative-critical alliance: 'The world was being made anew. Nothing, it seemed, had ever really been read'.[29]

At some time during the Kenyon episode, Lowell became a Roman Catholic. If Roman Catholicism and Marxism have been in our time the two major choices of intellectuals in search of an alternative to a sterile, bourgeois society, for Lowell it was

26. 'Visiting the Tates', in *Sewanee Review*, LXVII, Autumn 1959, pp. 557–9. There is an extended discussion of the relationship of the poetries of Tate and Lowell in R. K. Meiners, *Everything to be Endured: an essay on Robert Lowell and Modern Poetry*, Columbia (University of Missouri) 1970.

27. *Randall Jarrell 1914–1965*, New York (Farrar, Straus & Giroux) 1967, p. 103.

28. *P.R.*, p. 262.

29. *Ostroff*, p. 72.

symbolically a change of cities: Boston for Rome. Lowell has never expatiated at length on his conversion, but one obvious assumption is that the Catholic Church offered him more vital rituals, symbols and language than Boston's churches.[30] One critic has said: 'One can hardly avoid the conclusion that Lowell chose the Catholic Church as much to outrage his Calvinistic heritage as for any other reason'.[31] A poem such as 'At the Indian Killer's Grave' suggests another reason: the Catholic Church was not involved in the traditional sources of America's guilt about its failure to live up to its original promise. What *is* clear is that Lowell's Catholicism was short-lived, for the poems of *The Mills of the Kavanaughs* (1951) have loss of faith as a major theme, and 'Beyond the Alps', which first appeared in 1953, is a poem about more than a literal journey from Rome to Paris.

Lowell's commitment to political rebellion has been much more consistently maintained. The first public political act of his life was his refusal of conscription in 1943, which has become something of a literary *cause célèbre*, comparable to Arthur Miller's stand on McCarthyism. Considering Lowell's lifelong admiration for the military figure, with his unique combination of heroism, discipline and energies devoted to a public cause, it is hardly surprising that his attitude was not based on a pacifist total rejection of war; indeed, at the outbreak of the war, he had tried, unsuccessfully, to enlist in the navy. His poetry of the time displays war as both armageddon, and as capitalist apotheosis; but his objection to conscription was based on the Allies' demand for unconditional surrender, and on the mass bombings of the civilian population of Germany in 1943: the objection to mass

30. An influential American critic, Jerome Mazzaro, sees Lowell's career in what most readers of Lowell would perhaps regard as too strongly schematic Catholic terms. Briefly, he pictures Lowell as a poet whose early poetry is in a contemplative and meditative tradition, but whose later work has moved into a post-Christian world of 'lost religious purpose', 'absurdism' and 'irrational will'. (See Mazzaro's *The Poetic Themes of Robert Lowell*, and 'Lowell after *For the Union Dead*' in *London and Boyers*, pp. 84–97.) Grosvenor E. Powell, in 'Robert Lowell and Theodore Roethke: Two Kinds of Knowing', sees two traditions of mysticism: Christian and romantic. He includes Lowell in the former, alongside Donne and Eliot.

31. Will C. Jumper. 'Whom Seek Ye?', in *Parkinson*, pp. 59–60.

bombings is one he has maintained in relation to later wars.[32] In a letter to President Roosevelt, he brought up his family name but, with the kind of irony that has always played about Lowell's use of both military and family traditions, the family connection was thrown back in his face by the judge who tried his case: 'You are one of a distinguished family, and this will mar your family traditions.'[33] He received a sentence of a year and a day, of which he served five months. Little of Lowell's prison experience appears directly in his poetry, though it does produce two of his finest poems, 'In the Cage' and 'Memories of West Street and Lepke'; in the latter he describes himself memorably as a 'fire-breathing Catholic C.O.', reflecting his later sense of both the determined energies he had put into avoiding conscription, and his awareness of complicity largely through the violence of his early poetry and the endemic violence of New England's history, in the violence of war.

After the success of *Lord Weary's Castle* (1946), which won for Lowell a Pulitzer Prize, the late 'forties and early 'fifties were difficult years. *The Mills of the Kavanaughs* reflects in its tortuousness some crisis of both personality and aesthetic purpose. It marked the beginning of a lengthy period when Lowell published little, years of Senator McCarthy, the Cold War, the Eisenhower Administration, of the mental troubles recorded in 'Waking in the Blue', 'Home After Three Months Away' and 'Man and Wife', and of the deaths of Lowell's parents. In a phrase which has become almost a cliché of history, it was the 'tranquillized *Fifties*',[34] and Lowell's sense of the numbed shock endured by American liberals is conveyed by a poem which uses the traditional sonnet's rhetoric and the trappings of heroic poetry to give an ironic, deflating picture of Eisenhower's inauguration:

> Horseman, your sword is in the groove!
> Ice, ice. Our wheels no longer move;

32. In a symposium on 'The Cold War and the West', in *Partisan Review* XXIX, Winter 1962, p. 47, Lowell wrote: 'No nation should possess, use, or retaliate with its bombs. I believe we should rather die than drop our own bombs.'

33. Quoted in *Time*, LXXXIX, 22 June 1967, pp. 67–74.

34. *L.S.*, p. 99.

Look, the fixed stars, all just alike
as lack-land atoms, split apart,
and the Republic summons Ike,
the mausoleum in her heart.

('Inauguration Day: January 1953')

Lowell's career was taken up, and moved in a new direction, with the appearance of *Life Studies* in 1959. One of the most influential books of poetry of this century, it is the central text in the movement which has come to be known as 'Confessional Poetry'—one mainly associated with the names of Lowell, Sylvia Plath, Anne Sexton, W. D. Snodgrass and John Berryman. The phrase was probably first used by M. L. Rosenthal,[35] an American critic, in his characterisation of a trend towards a more naked poetry of personal concerns and honest exposure to experience, however harrowing the expression of them in poetry was for the poets concerned. Unfortunately, a term used as a suggestive counter became, in the way of these things, a label (like 'Theatre of the Absurd') that is neither precise nor, in the case of Lowell, comprehensive enough to convey the character of his work from *Life Studies* onwards. In recent years, it has often been used simply of the content of a poet's work. But applied in this way, it can be made to refer to work both formal and loose, remote and immediate, so as to make it virtually meaningless; it might equally well apply to Sir Walter Raleigh's poem written on the eve of his execution as to a Shelley lyric, and having the writer's personality the point of the whole proceedings is something Boswell and Rousseau would have understood. As a term applied to the effect of content on form it makes more sense, as a way of conveying how the special preoccupations of poets in our time have forced a new attitude both to the poet's audience, and to the poem as a self-contained art-object; in both cases, there is a new and special immediacy involved. Something like this is what Lowell has found in Sylvia Plath's poetry:

35. In his book, *The New Poets*, New York (O.U.P.) 1967, p. 25, M. L. Rosenthal writes: 'The term "confessional poetry" came naturally to my mind when I reviewed Robert Lowell's *Life Studies* in 1959, and perhaps it came to the minds of others just as naturally.'

In the best poems, one is torn by saying, 'This is so
true and lived that most other poetry seems like an
exercise,' and then one can back off and admire the
dazzling technique and invention. Perfect control, like
the control of a skier who avoids every death-trap until
reaching the final drop.[36]

(Like so much of Lowell's criticism of fellow-poets, it suggests
the way we should read his own poetry.) *Notebook* is his most
'confessional' book, if one simply looks for poetry that unfolds
its creator's life honestly and unashamedly. But *Life Studies* only
does this in a qualified way. Its artful construction, its holding
of past experience at arm's length, its use of a saving irony and
humour, its concern to put things in a context of general and
family history—so that the book is seriously blemished, as the
early English editions were, without the autobiographical '91
Revere Street'—mean that whatever of the private is offered is
subservient to the kind of concerns met with in most poetry.
(But even over this basic 'confessional' text, critics have tended
to fall out in an extreme way; whereas Rosenthal says, 'Lowell
removes the mask. His speaker is unequivocally himself, and it is
hard not to think of *Life Studies* as a series of personal confidences,
rather shameful, that one is honour-bound not to reveal'[37], another
critic, John Bayley, sees in *Life Studies* 'a drama without an
audience . . . the utter detachment of the mad'.[38] Both probably
exaggerate the extent to which Lowell has moved beyond
traditional attitudes to poem and audience.) 'Confession', for an
American poet, has some very traditional antecedents: in the
soul-searching of Puritan writing, and even in that most 'confessional' of poets, Walt Whitman (who once provoked G. H.
Lewes to protest: 'we deplore the unnecessary openness with
which Walt reveals to us matters which ought rather to remain
in a sacred silence'.)[39] But Lowell's particular kind of authority
in his personal poetry derives from his assumption that the

36. Letter to M. L. Rosenthal, quoted in *op. cit.*, p. 68.
37. *The Nation*, 19 September 1959, p. 154.
38. *London Magazine*, June 1966, p. 80.
39. Quoted on p. 209 of Kincheloe, *British Periodical Criticism of American
Literature, 1851–1870* (unpublished thesis, Duke University).

contours of his life, however unique and particularised, have a larger dimension; as Christopher Ricks says, 'The singular strength of Robert Lowell's poetry has always been a matter of his power to enforce a sense of context'.[40] Like Eliot and Yeats, he works to a sense of prior orders in the world: 'other things being equal it's better to get your emotions out in a Macbeth than in a confession'.[41]

Lowell's own criticism shows the wide range of his interests, and the many influences that have combined to shape him as a poet. Contained in poems, interviews and a comparatively small amount of prose, it includes appreciations of Eliot's 'Four Quartets', Hopkins, I. A. Richards as poet, translations of Ovid, John Berryman, Sylvia Plath, Randall Jarrell, Dylan Thomas, Elizabeth Bishop, Hart Crane and William Carlos Williams, and is distinguished by its unacademic liveliness, its creative poise and its generosity towards writers of persuasions other than his own. For Eliot, criticism was as 'inevitable as breathing', but if so much of the criticism industry sounds like a distinct kind of asphyxiation, the charge can't be brought against Lowell as critic. He has always been suspicious of academic criticism, and confesses: 'I'm very anxious in criticism not to do the standard analytical essay. I'd like my essay to be much sloppier and more intuitive.'[42] Of poets of an older generation, he has been particularly perceptive about William Carlos Williams, and has defined his peculiar genius well, and what he has meant for a younger writer working a very different seam. The history of Lowell's 'affair' with Williams is a fascinating one. As an undergraduate at Harvard he attempted verse in the Williams manner, but at Kenyon, found himself in the New Critics circle where Williams' work was not admired. Yet, over the years, he has functioned for Lowell as a way of absorbing such apparently alien influences as that of Pound, Whitman, the Imagists—and even Amy Lowell—so that Williams is a writer whom Lowell has had to 'make his pact with', as Pound did with Whitman, Williams' major precursor. How near Lowell's critical writings are to his own poetic practice can be seen in what must surely

40. *Price*, p. 97.
41. *P.R.*, p. 249.
42. *Op. cit.*, p. 241.

be the most unorthodox opening to a critical essay ever published in the *Hudson Review*:

> When I think about writing on Dr. Williams, I feel a chaos of thoughts and images, images cracking open to admit a thought, thoughts dragging their roots for the soil of an image. When I woke up this morning, something unusual for this summer was going on!— pinpricks of rain were falling in a reliable, comforting simmer. Our town was blanketed in the rain of rot and the rain of renewal. New life was muscling in, everything growing moved on its one-way trip to the ground. I could feel this, yet believe our universal misfortune was bearable and even welcome. An image held my mind during these moments and kept returning —an old fashioned New England cottage freshly painted white. I saw a shaggy, triangular shade on the house, trees, a hedge, or their shadows, the blotch of decay. The house might have been the house I was now living in, but it wasn't; it came from the time when I was a child, still unable to read and living in the small town of Barnstable on Cape Cod. Inside the house was a birdbook with an old stiff and steely engraving of a sharp-shinned hawk. The hawk's legs had a reddish brown buffalo fuzz on them; behind was the blue sky, bare and abstracted from the world. In the present, pinpricks of rain were falling on everything I could see, and even on the white house in my mind, but the hawk's picture, being indoors I suppose, was more or less spared. Since I saw the picture of the hawk, the pinpricks of rain have gone on, half the people I once knew are dead, half the people I now know were then unborn, and I have learned to read.[43]

(Readers of *For the Union Dead* will recognise the materials here of several poems; in particular, 'Eye and Tooth'.) How very

43. 'William Carlos Williams', in *Hudson Review*, XIV, Winter 1961–62, p. 530.

different all this is, in its complex strenuousness, from Williams' account of his poetic practice: 'I took the river as it followed its course down to the sea; all I had to do was follow it and I had a poem'.[44] Behind the different practices are different philosophies. Williams is supremely the poet of discovery who accepts the New World on its own terms, not the artist's, or the culture's; for him, history is something to get behind and before, for American history began with 'murder and enslavement, not with discovery'.[45] His special genius is to represent America in a native idiom, in poems which are 'movements', 'processes' and 'events', rather than finished art-objects.

Lowell's view of Williams is expressed with a mixture of affection and gentle ribbing: 'I can see him rushing from his practice to his typewriter, happy that so much of the world has rubbed off on him, maddened by its hurry.' The picture is so unlike our conception of Lowell at work that we take it as Lowell's strategy for defining differences in poetic character. Having gone to school with Tate and Ransom, poets who laboriously spent lifetimes in 'building up personal styles', Lowell is fascinated by Williams, whose poetic flowers 'rustle by the super-highways', and whose achievements are 'snatched up on the run': the very opposite of Lowell's own constant struggle to mate matter with form and to assimilate various traditions. Lowell sees Williams as perfectly at home in the American landscape, though one detects a touch of friendly condescension in Lowell's words: 'he loves America excessively, as if it were *the* truth and *the* subject'. Yet, though Williams' Paterson and Lowell's Boston are the fruits of very different poetic trees, Lowell's essay strangely affects the reader into believing that they share some common roots.

With the poetry from *Life Studies* onwards, Lowell increasingly unfolded the details of his private life. He has been married three times, and has a daughter and a son. His first marriage—to Jean Stafford, a writer—ended in divorce in 1948; its difficulties are charted in some of Lowell's marriage poems. His second marriage—to Elizabeth Hardwick, another writer—produced a daughter, Harriet; wife and daughter feature in

44. *I wanted to write a Poem*, London (Cape) 1967, p. 82.
45. *In the American Grain*, Norfolk, Conn. (New Directions) 1956, p. 39.

several of Lowell's most moving and successful poems. There is an uniquely warm and luminous innocence about the phrases he uses to describe his daughter:

> Blue-ribboned, blue-jeaned, named for you,
> our daughter cartwheels on the blue—[46]
>
> ('Fourth of July in Maine')

> Latin, Spanish, swimming half a mile,
> writing a saga with a hero named Eric,
> Latin, Spanish, math and rollerskates;
> a love of pretty dresses, but not boys.[47]
>
> ('Growth')

In the 1960's, Lowell moved to New York, which in the Naipaul interview, he refers to as the centre of contemporary American literary consciousness. It was the beginning of not only a period of continuous creativity, but also one of renewed political involvement. In the 'fifties, Lowell had supported Adlai Stevenson's doomed candidature for the Presidency; in the 'sixties, he welcomed J. F. Kennedy's election:

> Kennedy represents a side of America that's appealing
> to the artist in retrospect, a certain heroism. You feel
> in certain terms he really was a martyr in his death;
> that he was reckless, went further than the office
> called for, and perhaps that he was fated to be killed.
> That's an image one could treasure, and it stirs one.[48]

Stevenson and Kennedy were, of course, the kind of intellectuals who fascinate other intellectuals: very vulnerable figures, dogged by an heroic air of failure, or a sense of their own ineffectuality. As a member of what many Americans see as an élitist East Coast liberal establishment, Lowell was drawn into the famous Kennedy intellectual circle, but judging by his account of a White House dinner, must have reflected how sadly different

46. *N.O.*, p. 20.
47. *N.* p. 247.
48. *Alvarez*, pp. 39–40.

its cultural narcissism was from the Boston of 1830–60, when the poet could really feel he meant something in the larger world of politics:

> We all drank a great deal, and had to sort of be told
> not to take our champagne into the concert, to put
> our cigarettes out—like children—though nicely; it
> wasn't peremptory. Then the next morning you read
> that the Seventh Fleet had been sent somewhere in
> Asia and you had a funny feeling of how unimportant
> the artist really was: that this was sort of window-
> dressing and the real government was somewhere else,
> and that something much closer to the Pentagon was
> really ruling the country.[49]

The climax of his public political commitment to date was reached in 1967, with his participation in the Pentagon March, an event documented in both Lowell's own *Notebook*, with its strong political current, and in Norman Mailer's *The Armies of the Night*.

'Justice is strife, and war the father of gods':[50] Lowell has always been a pessimistic political animal. In his political actions and comments in recent years there is a sense of accelerating hopelessness: at the quixotics of political behaviour, at the un-willingness of nations to embrace internationalism, at the inability of the ordinary man-in-the-street to influence the course of events, at the absence of a Lincoln ('our most noble and likable president'[51]) in a patently divided nation, at the loss of a series of liberal leaders in Adlai Stevenson, Eugene McCarthy and John F. Kennedy, at the erosion of faith and confidence in American life,[52] and at a sense of personal isolation in a world of super powers, and less than super politicians. Lowell's class has been doubly rejected: by the 'silent majority' for its 'snobbery', and by the radical Left, for its ineffectual liberalism. The par-ticular value of Mailer's portrait of Lowell in *The Armies of the*

49. *Ibid.*, p. 40.
50. *N.*, p. 142.
51. 'What's happening to America', in *Partisan Review*, XXXIV, 1967, p. 38.
52. See *Encounter*, May 1973, p. 67.

Night is that, though it leans heavily on the slack 'profile' clichés of Sunday newspaper journalism, it is informed by a sympathetic understanding of Lowell's well-meaning political beleaguerement. New York Jewish novelist meets Boston, Beacon Hill poet in circumstances where the first is at home, the second poignantly ill-at-ease; after Mailer himself, Lowell is this 'Novel as History' 's hero:

> Lowell has the expression on his face of a dues payer who is just about keeping up with the interest on some enormous debt. As he sits on the floor with his long arms clasped mournfully about his long Yankee legs, 'I am here,' says his expression, 'but I do not pretend I like what I see.' The hollows in his cheeks give a hint of the hanging judge. Lowell is of good weight, not too heavy, not too light, but the hollows speak of the great Puritan gloom in which the country was founded—man was simply not good enough for God.[53]

In many ways, Lowell's career to date suggests an agonised Prometheus tied to a rock of tragic contemporary experience. But, as the ending of 'The Exile's Return' has it: 'Your life is in your hands'.[54] Now, in the 1970's, he is living in England, divorced from Elizabeth Hardwick, after twenty-five years of marriage, and married to Caroline Blackwood, by whom he has a son: the story is told in *For Lizzie and Harriet* (1973) and *The Dolphin* (1973). But the urge for survival is as fierce as ever, after a lifetime of careful plotting to-and-fro between the shores of exile and return to the sources of his poetry in American history, Boston and New England.

53. *The Armies of the Night*, London (Penguin), p. 43.
54. *P.*, p. 13.

2 This Imperfect Globe

One obvious launching-pad for a survey of Lowell's early poetry is his own account of his poetic beginnings in the *Paris Review* interview. However, the interview is available in several collections of criticism,[1] and readers whose initial interest has been aroused by Lowell's poetry will no doubt want to read it for themselves; moreover, the special attractions of a poet's hindsight on his own work are no substitute for his immediate responses at the time of the poems' composition, and particularly, his early reactions to other poets. And in Lowell's case, there is a more-than-ordinary interest about his criticism of this early period; two cases in point are his review of Eliot's 'Four Quartets',[2] and his 'Note' on Hopkins' poetry.[3]

In 1943, Lowell reviewed 'Four Quartets' enthusiastically, and found it 'one of the very few great poems in which craftsmanship and religious depth are equal'. In Eliot's 'wrestling with language, artistic craft [was] analogous to contemplative discipline, aesthetic experience . . . to extasy', and the product of these disciplines was 'a composite of the symbolic, the didactic, and the confessional'. But the aspect of the poem Lowell draws most attention to is its unified vision: the key words of his review are 'union', 'composite', 'integration', 'unity' and 'community'. Something similar accounts for the impact Hopkins has on him. In his 'Note' of 1944, he sees Hopkins' poetry as 'substantially dramatic', and of 'the whole-man', as opposed to others' poetry of a 'single faculty'. (In the *Paris Review* interview, the latter sentiment recurs in relation to Hart Crane: 'There was a fullness of experience . . . the push of the whole man is there.'[4])

1. See Select Bibliography.
2. 'A Review of "Four Quartets" ', in *Sewanee Review*, LI, Summer 1943, pp. 432–5.
3. 'A Note' (on Hopkins), in *Kenyon Review*, VI, Autumn 1944, pp. 583–6.
4. *P.R.*, p. 264.

These views of Eliot and Hopkins are worth pondering, for they establish that some of the guide-lines for Lowell's later career were sketched early on, and they account for the dramatic sweep and 'wrestling with language' of his first two published poems, of which the following is typical:

> Cancer ossifies his features,
> The starved skeleton shows its teeth,
> Flamingo crackling embroiders
> Italian bones with shameless froth.[5]

Rhythmically, these lines do little to recall Hopkins, but there is, nevertheless, a touch of that rabid, didactic push of certain passages of 'The Wreck of the Deutschland':

> But Gertrude, lily, and Luther, are two of a town,
> Christ's lily and beast of the waste wood:
> From life's dawn it is drawn down,
> Abel is Cain's brother and breasts they have sucked the same.[6]

Usually, the element of Hopkins in Lowell's early verse is mated to the kind of gnarled lyricism Crane exhibits in a poem such as 'To Brooklyn Bridge', but both poets suggested to Lowell a way of getting a harsh energy of movement into a poetry of lyric forms, and of injecting it with drama. If Eliot's presence in Lowell's lines above is only a ghostly one, this has something to do with Lowell's admiration for Tate and Ransom. One of the things that impressed the young poet about these two was the appearance of sustained effort about their work: 'an attempt to make poetry much more formal than Eliot and Pound, to write in metres but to make the metres look hard and make them hard to write'.[7]

Lowell's first book—*Land of Unlikeness*—appeared in 1944 (in a limited edition of 250 copies) with an Introduction by Tate, and its twenty-one poems are the fruits of the apprenticeship

5. 'The Cities' Summer Death', in *Kenyon Review*, I, Winter 1939, p. 32.

6. 'The Wreck of the Deutschland', p. 19 of Penguin edition of Hopkins.

7. Interview with A. Alvarez, 'Robert Lowell in Conversation', in *The Review*, 8, August 1963, pp. 38–9.

briefly sketched above. On the book's cover, Cross and gargoyle meet: an apt confrontation for a book in which Yeats's 'blood-dimmed tide' sweeps across a landscape of outrage, war, catastrophe and violence. The title of the book (from St. Bernard) recalls Eliot's 'The Waste Land': the world is a place of exile and banishment for the poet-prophet, in which man has lost his perception of his soul's likeness to God. In a charged response to abandoned New England traditions, the Second World War, and alienation from God in a capitalist society, the book sees man as either poised agonisingly between the worlds of myth and monster, animal and angel, or operating in a world irredeemably given over to secular pursuits. In one poem, Christ is 'for sale';[8] in another, there is an alliance between the mass media and capitalism, between religion and totalitarianism:

> Here the stamped tabloid, ballot, draft or actress
> Consumes all access and all faculties
> For spreading blandishments or terror. Here
> Puppets have heard the civil words of Darwin
> Clang clang, while the divines of screen and air
> Twitter like Virgil's harpies eating plates,
> And lions scamper up the rumps of sheep[9]

—a description of Nazi Germany, it might, with a few alterations, do duty as an account of wartime democratic America. Frequent parallels are drawn between contemporary places and events, and those in history and the Bible: Christ is a stillborn child in Boston; Boston's Charles River is the Acheron; war is an Abel-Cain conflict; and the world exists in the long shadow of Adam's Fall. Full of a Revelatory imagery of Leviathan, dragon, serpent and lion, the poems tend to be all climax—except where there is a temporary proffering of salvation. Not surprisingly, Lowell shares many of the styles and techniques of his early poetry with the New Apocalypse writers of the forties collected in the 1941 anthology *The White Horseman*;[10] but

8. 'Christ for Sale', in *L.U.*
9. 'Cistercians in Germany', in *L.U.*
10. *The White Horseman*, ed. J. F. Hendry and Henry Treece, London (Routledge) 1941.

he gives his poems a quite individual push in the direction o
caricature and lampoon:

> So, Child, unclasp your fists
> And clap for Freedom and Democracy[11]

> Charon's raft / Dumps its damned goods into the
> harbour-bed.[12]

With its surge of sarcasm and snarl, of judgement rather than
understanding, the colloquialisms, slang, savage puns, and
vulgar ironies seem techniques to engage the reader, but the
frequent rhetorical questions, refrains and repetitions, apostrophes, and complex stanza forms seem intended either to hold
the reader at a distance, or repel him.

The poems of *Land of Unlikeness* are mainly religious dramas
with Adam and Eve, Cain and Abel, Mammon and Leviathan
Mars and Bellona, Satan, Christ and Mary as the protagonists
and with Boston, New England and Nazi Germany as the stage
settings. In his Introduction, Tate talked of Lowell as specifically
a Catholic poet, and many early reviewers saw him as something
like a more energetic and technically-minded Thomas Merton.[13]
In a particularly acute way, Lowell's poetry on religious theme
resurrects the old problem of the relation between belief and
art: it is not easy to be sure, when one is praising or deploring
the 'art' of a particular passage, that it is not the 'belief' one is
attending to. Yet Time clarifies some things, and few reader
would now go along with John Berryman's view of Lowell as
'the master of a freedom in the Catholic subject without peer
since Hopkins'.[14] In these early poems, Catholic theology consort
uneasily with the world-view of the Puritan New Englander—
innate depravity, damnation, and a continuous soul-searching—
and many of Lowell's lines give one the frisson of being at a

11. 'Song of the Boston Nativity', in *Partisan Review*, X, July–August 1943
pp. 316–7; also in *L.U.*, under the title 'The Boston Nativity'.
12. *P.*, p. 36.
13. Thus, J. F. Nims, in his review of *Land of Unlikeness*, in *Poetry*, LXV
1944–45, pp. 264–8; and Howard Moss, in his review of *Lord Weary's Castl*
in *Kenyon Review*, IX, 1947, pp. 290–8.
14. 'Lowell, Thomas, etc.', in *Partisan Review*, XIV, 1947, pp. 73–85.

revival meeting in a great medieval cathedral. The poems' surface complication, and proliferation of references and objects, place Lowell nearer to certain decadent metaphysical poets, than to Hopkins: Crashaw, for the steamed-up physicality ('Christ the Drunkard brews / Gall, or spiked bone-vat, siphons His bilged blood'[15]), and Edward Taylor, for the ungainly metaphors ('O Mother, I implore / Your scorched, blue thunderbreasts of love to pour / Buckets of blessings on my burning head'[16]). If the Catholic stance in these poems suggests that of the convert who sees his fellow, unconverted men in a state of spiritual deprivation, these are not poems of devotion and faith, for there is no individual possession of religion—except that one feels Lowell is externalising his personal conflicts. An example is the ending of 'Dea Roma', which seems infused with a satirical glee at religious degeneration, and makes the comment on this poem by one critic that it 'reenforces Catholicism as a condition for salvation'[17] seem besides the point. A series of basic contradictions in Lowell's approach to religious themes often has the effect of dumping the poems in a sea of rhetoric: the Calvinism stresses violence and confusion, and convinces us of unavoidable depravity and doom, the Catholicism tries to persuade us of the availability of a grace, salvation and redemption that will free us. But the only Christian experience that Lowell seems able to contemplate in the present is one of violence, and we never see the workings of grace in people or things. When he wants to present a positive Christianity, he often pictures it as a simple withdrawal of energy.

In his Introduction, Tate also suggested that Lowell's symbolic language had the effect of being 'willed'. An overdose of symbols often clogs up the works:

> Bring me tonight no axe to grind
> On wheels of the Utopian mind:
>   Six thousand years
> Cain's blood has drummed into my ears,

15. 'Christ for Sale', in *L.U.*
16. *P.*, p. 32.
17. Jerome Mazzaro, in *The Poetic Themes of Robert Lowell*, p. 32.

ROBERT LOWELL

> Shall I wring plums from Plato's bush
> When Burma's and Bizerte's dead
> Must puff and push
> Blood into bread?[18]

What mainly comes across here—apart from the very stiff treatment of a complex form—is a whirl of transitions: Utopia . . . Cain . . . Plato . . . Burma . . . the Mass . . . are held in some sort of relation, but it is not one that convinces us there is any depth to the poem's statement. Rather than engaging our responses, the colloquial first line, and the energetic verbs, merely force a conviction that there is no still centre of the turbulent world of the poem, and that the lack of restraint testifies both to Lowell's youth, and to some failure of the imagination: the energy which creates the vision of an emblematic world of spiritual struggle is negating the clear-sightedness needed for its expression. In this connection, it is worth quoting at length from R. P. Blackmur's summing-up of *Land of Unlikeness*:

> . . . Lowell's verse is a beautiful case of citation in any
> argument in support of the belief in the formal
> inextricability of the various elements of poetry:
> meter is not meter by itself, any more than attitude
> or anecdote or perception, though any one of them
> can be practised by itself at the expense of the others,
> when the tensions become mere fanaticism of spirit
> and of form: conditions, one would suppose, mutually
> mutilating. Something of that sort seems to be
> happening in Lowell's verse. It is as if he demanded to
> *know* (to judge, to master) both the substance apart
> from the form with which he handles it and the form
> apart from the substance handled in order to set them
> fighting . . . Lowell is distraught about religion; he
> does not seem to have decided whether his Roman
> Catholic belief is the form of a force or the sentiment
> of a form. The result seems to be that in dealing with
> men his faith compels him to be fractiously vindictive,

18. 'On the Eve of the Feast of the Immaculate Conception, 1942', in *Sewanee Review*, LI, Summer 1943, pp. 393–4; also in *L.U.*

and in dealing with faith his experience of men compels him to be nearly blasphemous. By contrast, Dante loved his living Florence and the Florence to come and loved much that he was compelled to envisage in hell, and he wrote throughout in loving meters. In Lowell's *Land of Unlikeness* there is nothing loved unless it be its repellence; and there is not a loving meter in the book. What is thought of as Boston in him fights with what is thought of as Catholic; and the fight produces not a tension but a gritting. It is not the violence, the rage, the denial of this world that grits, but the failure of these to find *in verse* a tension of necessity; necessity has, when recognised, the quality of conflict accepted, not hated. If Lowell, like St. Bernard whom he quotes on his title page, conceives the world only as a place of banishment, and poetry (or theology) only as a means of calling up memories of life before banishment, he has the special problem of maturing a medium . . . in which vision and logic combine . . . the poems themselves suggest . . . that he has so far been able to express only the violence of its difficulty.[19]

In the compilation of his next book—*Lord Weary's Castle*—Lowell, in his own words, 'took out several [poems] that were paraphrases of early Christian poems, and I rejected one rather dry abstraction, then whatever seemed to me to have a messy violence. All the poems have religious imagery, I think, but the ones I took were more concrete. That's what the book was moving toward: less symbolic imagery.'[20] The new book's title refers to a ballad story on the theme of man's ingratitude, with a mythical extension in the rejection of Christ.[21] As the individual poems' titles indicate, the prevailing season is winter, but spring round the corner, the possibilities for new life and individual salvation are strongly felt. Another major development is that

19. 'Notes on Seven Poets', in *Language as Gesture*, pp. 352–63.
20. *P.R.*, p. 243.
21. There are interesting interpretations of the title by John Berryman, in *Partisan Review*, XIV; and by W. C. Jumper, in *Hudson Review*, IX.

there is now less of the explicit attack on capitalism, though it is a strong feature of 'To Peter Taylor on the Feast of the Epiphany'. Certain earlier lines and phrases—such as, 'the price-controller's stranglehold',[22] the 'venery of Capital',[23] and 'Yankee laissez-faire and enterprise'[24]—seemed largely to reflect the agrarian views of the Southern Fugitives, and lack the pressure of individual conviction.

In general, Lowell's poems are now more personal, more localised, and more related to specific historical events; and yet, paradoxically, they work with a sharper edge of universality. Several of the new book's poems on religious themes—'Christmas Eve under Hooker's Statue'; 'Colloquy in Black Rock'; 'The Holy Innocents'; 'The First Sunday in Lent'—show a considerable progress towards that 'tension of necessity' which Blackmur found largely lacking in Lowell's earliest poetry, and with the poems which relate the Christian experience to that of war, Lowell takes his place alongside other important American poets of the Second World War experience, such as Randall Jarrell, James Dickey, Richard Wilbur, Louis Simpson and Anthony Hecht. The vital difference, of course, is that Lowell was a noncombatant: without using the properties of war poetry, such as concentration camps and atomic weapons, he sees war as an extension of history's unholy alliances, which place Leviathan's worldly power at the service of man's innate violence: 'How can / War ever change my old into new man?'[25] (On the title-page of *Lord Weary's Castle*, the illustration is of Cain's killing of Abel.)

'Colloquy in Black Rock' relates only indirectly to the war, but shows how this can be done successfully. A celebration of the Feast of Corpus Christi, and of St. Stephen, it makes effective use of a particular locale, and is in the form of a 'colloquy' between Lowell and his 'heart'. The opening recalls Hopkins' 'terrible sonnets', and has something of the clogged *Land of*

22. 'Christmas Eve in the Time of War', in *L.U.*
23. 'The Capitalist's Meditation by the Civil War Monument, Christmas, 1942', in *Partisan Review*, X, July–August 1943, pp. 314–5; also in *L.U.* in revised version.
24. 'Prayer for the Jews', in *Sewanee Review*, LI, Summer 1943, p. 395.
25. *P.*, p. 59.

Unlikeness manner, but Lowell's energies are now made sub-servient to the form, rather than pushing it along, and the rhythms are firmer and related to the Bridgeport industrial scene. Indeed, the form of this poem is quite an achievement, consisting of something like an anthem, with alternate sestets and quatrains of statements and refrains. And Lowell has found a suitable analogy between outer and inner worlds of violence, and between secular and religious, in the jackhammer/heart analogy. As in other poems in *Lord Weary's Castle* about feast days, there is the appearance of a God of salvation at the poem's end, and a quiet, sustained resolution, which contrasts markedly with the opening:

> Christ walks on the black water. In Black Mud
> Darts the Kingfisher. On Corpus Christi, heart,
> Over the drum-beat of St. Stephen's choir
> I hear him, *Stupor Mundi,* and the mud
> flies from his hunching wings and beak—my heart,
> The blue kingfisher dives on you in fire.[26]

'Colloquy in Black Rock' is one of several poems of religious rhetoric in the book which are qualified successes; but the tradition of which they are a part, and which, taken to an apo-calyptic extreme, produces such poems as 'As a Plane Tree by the Water' and 'Where the Rainbow Ends', is one continually on the brink of stylistic disasters. Its faults are those which Lowell found in Hopkins' poetry: 'in some poems we feel that the intensity is mannered, in others we could wish for more variety . . . infrequently his lines collapse in a styleless exuber-ance'.[27] Ultimately, there seems more lasting achievement in the less ambitious poems on religious themes, such as 'The Holy Innocents' and 'The First Sunday in Lent'. The first is an evenly-paced pastoral anecdote with Breughel-like touches:

> Listen, the hay-bells tinkle as the cart
> Wavers on rubber tires along the tar
> And cindered ice below the burlap mill

26. *P.,* p. 15.
27. 'A Note', in *Kenyon Review,* VI, Autumn 1944, pp. 585–6.

And ale-wife run. The oxen drool and start
In wonder at the fenders of a car,
And blunder hugely up St. Peter's hill.[28]

The second, before it passes into successive stages of Eliotic
'confessional' and visionary poetry, marvellously evokes a Lenten
harshness:

The crooked family chestnut sighs, for March,
Time's fool, is storming up and down the town;
The gray snow squelches and the well-born stamp
From sermons in a scolded, sober mob
That wears away the Sabbath with a frown,
A world below my window.[29]

Several poems in *Lord Weary's Castle* take Boston as their
locale, a Boston often caught in the throes of some disaster; and
the poems state the price for survival. But the book's finest
poem on a city-theme is about a European city. As the opening
poem of the book, 'The Exile's Return' is partly an invocation
to the reader. Its heavily-bourgeois city is both a mythical
extension of Boston and of the destroyed Lord Weary's castle
and an American-occupied Rhineland city, but with enough
carefully-placed allusions to give it a general European flavour.
It is undergoing post-war recovery, an arctic half-life, and the
opening conveys a physically-ambiguous existence—

There mounts in squalls a sort of rusty mire,
Not ice, not snow, to leaguer the Hôtel
De Ville, where braced pig-iron dragons grip
The blizzard to their rigor mortis[30]

—which is translated into spiritual terms at the end of the poem.
With a title recalling Malcolm Cowley's influential book about
modern artist-exiles,[31] and using details from Mann's 'Tonio
Kröger',[32] the poem posits exile as the condition of the modern

28. *P.*, p. 14.   29. *P.*, p. 25.   30. *P.*, p. 13.
31. *Exile's Return: a literary Odyssey of the 1920's*, New York (Viking Press) 1951.
32. Philip Cooper, in *The Autobiographical Myth of Robert Lowell*, pp. 48–51,
traces in some detail the relationship between Mann's story and Lowell's poem.

artist—Joyce, Lawrence, Conrad—and Lowell himself, self-exiled from Boston's traditions, and from the war which produced the 'land of unlikeness' described in the poem. The exile returning to his 'gray, sorry and ancestral house' is the artist as displaced person of the spirit, who must find release from his imprisonment in shaping his own life, and in an acceptance of the despiritualised world of modern man:

> already lily-stands
> Burgeon the risen Rhineland, and a rough
> Cathedral lifts its eye. Pleasant enough,
> *Voi ch'entrate*, and your life is in your hands.[33]

The balance in these lines between part of Dante's inscription over the entrance to Hell ('Lasciate ogui speranza, voi ch'entrate': 'Abandon all hope, ye who enter'), and images of Spring and rebirth, suggests the qualified optimism with which Lowell views his own life, and the post-war world. And in the use of Mann and Dante, and in the all-encompassing figure of the exile—Christ, artist, displaced person, a Jonathan Edwards and Hawthorne of post-war Europe—Lowell has achieved a rare kind of universality.

On the evidence of 'The Exile's Return' and other poems of *Lord Weary's Castle*, it would seem that Lowell's view of Boston and of the Second World War, and of some proffered salvation is at its most moving when grounded in some literary precedent, some personal or family 'plot', or in a worked-out view of American (particularly New England) history. The vision that produces such poems as 'Salem', 'Concord', 'The Quaker Graveyard in Nantucket', 'At the Indian Killer's Grave' and 'In Memory of Arthur Winslow' is no less racked than that of the 'prophetic' poems. But in each case, Lowell has taken personal possession of a piece of New England history, in a manner which recalls Jarrell's words: 'His present contains the past . . . as an operative skeleton just under the skin.'[34] They show that Lowell is a more convincing poet when he is examining the endemic corruption of Puritan stock from the beginning, than when, as in

33. *P.*, p. 13.
34. 'The Kingdom of Necessity', in *London and Boyers*, p. 23.

Land of Unlikeness, he is obsessed with a corruption in the present. For each poem, he has found an appropriate form for that possession—sonnet, elegy, a complex 'metaphysical' stanza, couplets with short-line variations, and a mixture of couplets and stanzas. In a way, they are minor masterpieces of formal ingenuity.

The most celebrated of all Lowell's treatments of New England's violent and contradictory past is 'The Quaker Graveyard in Nantucket'. This poem has been analysed at length by several critics,[35] so perhaps a brief glance at some of the issues the poem raises is in order here. Dedicated to a Winslow cousin killed at sea in the Second World War, the 'Quaker Graveyard' explores the capacity for violence in man and nature which has produced the death. The violence of man against man in war is seen as related to that prideful, Ahab-like struggle for dominion over nature, and to the old Calvinist belief in the superiority of the Elect. So the poem is both a critique of universal man's assumption of self-sufficiency as the originator of his own moral order, and a working-out of the terms of God's promise to man of dominion over the natural world; and the poem ultimately restores man to that middle state—'upward angel, downward fish'—his pride has usurped. Whether this exploration of the trinity of God-man-nature comes across with the single-minded, point-for-point correspondence of symbol, language and structure the poem's admirers stress, is another matter. A case has been made out for the poem as a re-working of a traditional form, the elegy,[36] and there are certainly suggestions of this in the set-piece passages of denunciation and incantation; and there is plenty of evidence of Lowell's careful introduction of structuring motifs and verbal echoes into each of the poem's seven sections. Yet, in spite of all this, one senses a lack of development, and a circling round certain ideas and motifs, and there is the controversial sixth section ('Our Lady of Walsingham') to come to terms with. Structurally, this latter section effects a transition

35. For example, Patrick Cosgrave, in *The Public Poetry of Robert Lowell*; Paul J. Dolan, 'Lowell's "Quaker Graveyard": Poem and Tradition', in *Renascence*, XXI, 1969, pp. 171–80, 194; and *Staples*.

36. By Marjorie Perloff, 'Death by Water: The Winslow Elegies of Robert Lowell', in *Journal of English Literary History*, XXXIV, March 1967, pp. 116–40.

between the violence of the first five sections, and the view of a wind-swept graveyard in the last, and is something like the 'consolation' passage in a traditional elegy. But thematically, it jars: its view of an 'expressionless', withdrawn deity in an English pastoral setting seems as much a manifestation of an exclusive religion as the one it opposes in the poem, and the denial of a grace available at all—though it is difficult to see how otherwise Lowell could prepare for the last section's vision of death and the re-assertion of God's will. Ultimately, one admires the poem as a tour-de-force exhibition of a modern rhetoric of the sea:

> Sailor, can you hear
> The Pequod's sea wings, beating landward, fall
> Headlong and break on our Atlantic wall
> Off 'Sconset, where the yawing S-boats splash
> The bellbuoy, with ballooning spinnakers,
> As the entangled, screeching mainsheet clears
> The blocks: off Madaket, where lubbers lash
> The heavy surf and throw their long lead squids
> For blue-fish? Sea-gulls blink their heavy lids
> Seaward.[37]

Contrast that with this wholly different passage, with its desolate, unheroic music:

> Let the sea-gulls wail
>
> For water, for the deep where the high tide
> Mutters to its hurt self, mutters and ebbs.
> Waves wallow in their wash, go out and out,
> Leave only the death-rattle of the crabs,
> The beach increasing, its enormous snout
> Sucking the ocean's side.[38]

For passages like these, Lowell's poetry takes its rightful place with those other religious poems of the sea, 'The Wreck of the Deutschland' and Eliot's 'The Dry Salvages'.

37. *P.*, p. 19.
38. *P.*, p. 21.

For a more sustained treatment of New England's history, and a more deeply-integrative use of literary sources, many readers will turn to the two Jonathan Edwards poems, 'Mr. Edwards and the Spider' and 'After the Surprising Conversions'.[39] In his early days, Lowell started to write a book about Edwards, but then allowed his admiration for Edwards to express itself in poetry, rather than in straightforward biography. Lowell's feeling for Edwards is for a man of intense personality, a firm believer in the Calvinist theology of death, destruction, punishment and guilt who stuck to his beliefs in a time of religious apathy, and a man whose logical mind was racked by the paradox that belief often leads to an excess of spirit that spills over into death; in both poems, man's bleak apotheosis is contrasted with the abundance of nature at autumn time:

> In latter August when the hay
> Came creaking to the barn.[40]

> the bough cracks with the unpicked apples.[41]

In both poems, Edwards is the speaker, and his subject is the conversion of his uncle, Josiah Hawley, and its consequences; and it is a considerable achievement on Lowell's part to convince us that this is really Edwards' voice speaking, in a casual weave of historical fact, self-analysis and commentary, which uses the actual words of the adult Edwards, and of Edwards as an eleven-year-old boy. In 'Mr. Edwards and the Spider', the two sides of the historical Edwards—the boy-naturalist and the preacher—come together in a disquisition on the difference between animal and human approaches to death. The stanza-form, which one critic[42] sees as derived from Donne's 'A Nocturnal Upon St. Lucy's Day', could hardly be more appropriate: within its restrictive, but logically-inevitable framework, the

39. Dallas E. Wiebe has an article on the two Edwards poems in *Lord Weary's Castle*: 'Mr Lowell and Mr Edwards', in *Contemporary Literature*, 3, Spring-Summer 1962, pp. 21–31.

40. *P.*, p. 69.

41. *P.*, p. 72.

42. *Staples*, p. 35.

firm, albeit hell-fire, convictions of the preacher achieve a mastery over the boy's sense of wonder at the spiders' 'purposeless' lives, and meaningless deaths. The poem ends with a statement that echoes Yeats:

> this is death, to die and know it.[43]

(Both Edwards poems also anticipate the terms of Lowell's admiration for Sylvia Plath's 'imaginative risk',[44] and the very last phrase of 'Mr. Edwards and the Spider'—'This is the Black Widow, death'—is uncannily prophetic of her poetic voice.)

The second Edwards poem—'After the Surprising Conversions' —traces the consequences of Josiah Hawley's conversion, in his suicide and the arousal of the townspeople into a state of suicidal frenzy. The poem is in the form of a letter, in which Edwards attempts to produce a convincing doctrinal explanation of these events. Again, form and theme are in perfect conjunction. The regular couplets and firm, masculine rhymes mirror Edwards' will to fit everything to a theological framework, but the free letter-form, and the incessant use of run-over lines, act like a subversive counter-tow to the flow of Edwards' logic, as if the speaker is more than half-aware of the paradoxes he is conjuring with. Like its companion poem, it is successful largely because Lowell's voice speaks in Edwards through a mask that engages the poet at a human and natural level, and finds a perfect foil in the language of Edwards' sermons, essays and letters. In this respect, it is worth insisting on the importance of the many 'imitations', or poems 'after' a literary or pictorial original, in *Lord Weary's Castle*. Compared to 'Quaker Graveyard' or 'Where the Rainbow Ends', poems like 'War', 'Charles the Fifth and the Peasant', 'The Shako', 'France', '1790', 'The Blind Leading the Blind' and 'The Fens' seem unambitious and ordinary; but there is an unclotted, cut-away air about their style, a secular and painterly use of details and effects, and a return to the considerable virtues of straightforward narrative sweep and syntax that was important for Lowell's future:

43. *P.*, p. 70.
44. Letter to M. L. Rosenthal, quoted in M. L. Rosenthal, *The New Poets*, p. 68

A land of mattocks; here the brothers strode,
Hulking as horses in their worsted hose
And cloaks and shin-guards—each had hooked his hoe
Upon his fellow's shoulder; by each nose
The aimless waterlines of eyeballs show
Their greenness.[45]

It is of some significance that Lowell should have chosen the stripped, naturalistic honesty of Breughel and Cobbett for two of the best 'imitations'—'The Blind Leading the Blind' and 'The Fens', respectively. Anyone interested in the thought-processes of a poet at work on his raw materials could do no better than compare point-to-point the Cobbett passage in his *Rural Rides* with Lowell's poem, and the passage in Baron Thiebault's memoirs that inspired '1790'.[46] The immediate way ahead for Lowell after these fine historical cameos was to come to engage with contemporary experience, via a marriage of these poems' qualities to the creation of a special type of fictional character (one with an existence independent of his or her creator, yet also functioning as a projection of the poet's inner conflicts), the exploration of interior, psychological reality, and the mixing of different modes—naturalism, melodrama and surrealism, for example. 'Between the Porch and the Altar' and 'The Death of the Sheriff' are initial forays in this direction, but the most thorough-going treatment is in Lowell's third book, *The Mills of the Kavanaughs*.

Consisting of seven longish poems, *The Mills of the Kavanaughs* is the most difficult of all Lowell's books to date, and possibly the most underrated, though the idiom is not a totally unfamiliar one: a stoic New England dramatic monologue of family and marital quarrels, loneliness, madness and suicide. To this tradition belong the narrative poems of Frost, Randall Jarrell, and, in particular, Edwin Arlington Robinson's poetry of 'the blasted thoroughfares of disillusion' and 'scarred hopes outworn'.[47] In

45. *P.*, p. 74.
46. William Cobbett, *Rural Rides*, Vol. 2, London (Dent), 1930, p. 239; *The Memoirs of Baron Thiebault*, Vol. 1, tr. Arthur J. Butler, London (Smith, Elder), 1896, pp. 89–90.
47. Edwin Arlington Robinson, *Collected Poems*, New York (Macmillan) 1967, pp. 519 and 574, respectively.

retrospect, the poems of *The Mills of the Kavanaughs* can be seen to anticipate *Life Studies'* trapped minds and lives, failed family traditions, frustrated marriages and loves, and their themes of guilty love, incest, and adultery surface again in *Phaedra*. But simply to see the book like this does it an injustice. Though it lacks the surface verbal excitement of *Lord Weary's Castle*, and the plots are often (needlessly?) obscure, there are compensations. One of them is that, freed from the single-minded obsessions of the earlier books, Lowell works by multi-focus and perspective; another is that the poems use detail charged with the disturbing clarity of dream and nightmare; and thirdly, they are very scenic poems, and long after one has given up puzzling over their obscurities, one recalls their moving views of New York in winter, Concord, New Brunswick and Maine. But perhaps their greatest achievement is in the creation of character and plot. In the book's major poems, the speaker or protagonist pursues a love-starved life, unsustained by family, religious or historical traditions, and imprisoned by incest, family quarrels, or loss of faith, from which the only 'liberation' is into suicide, madness, reverie or world-liness. In these poems of reminiscence, dream and introspection, of psychological and religious conflicts mythicised, we overhear monologues by trapped consciousnesses, monologues without an audience: the lonely figure of Anne Kavanaugh playing solitaire hovers over the book, and seems some final secularised version of the Puritan self-tormenting mind. Either opposed to the Church, or unable to savour its consolations, the protagonists wish themselves outside history ('He thinks the past is settled'[48]), or in control of their own destinies ('Life is a thing I own'[49]); yet their reality is to be caught in the vagaries of memories, a prey to the attractions and destructions of worldly, amoral, sometimes aristocratic, existence, and to see their love given over to death ('Brother, try, O Child of Aphrodite, try to die: to die is life';[50] 'I gave Whatever brought me gladness to the grave'[51]). Reflecting a general trend in poetry after the war from social themes towards a psychological-cum-mythological mode, *The Mills of the Kavanaughs* is an attempt by Lowell to mediate

48. *P.*, p. 51; this is actually from a poem in *Lord Weary's Castle*, 'Between the Porch and the Altar'.

49. *P.*, p. 86.   50. *P.*, p. 82.   51. *M.K.*, p. 21.

personal experience and problems via third person poetic voices and classical myths, particularly the Persephone myth of seasonal renewal. This suggests the secular drift of Lowell's poetry, for pagan myths are now, to a large extent, divorced from Christian symbolism ('We were friends of Cato, not of God'[52]). The demands of humanity and of religion are in conflict, with the dead rituals of the Church, whether Catholic or Puritan, opposed to the love the characters hunger for ('The Douay Bible . . . Is *SOL*, her dummy'[53]).

However, in spite of these general common characteristics, the poems are surprisingly varied, and interesting in different ways, and several are among the best Lowell has written. 'Falling Asleep over the Aeneid' is a dream poem which uses strange metamorphoses, collage effects, vivid colours in a powerful brew of mythical, public and personal elements. Sharing some of the characteristics of the protagonist of Eliot's 'Gerontion', the old man of the poem is a sad survivor from a distinguished past of Civil War glories and Concord intellectual traditions. On a Sunday morning in Concord, he misses going to church by falling asleep, and dreams himself into the passage of the Aeneid (about Pallas' funeral) he has been reading, and on waking, recalls a childhood incident when he was sent to bed whilst reading Vergil. The Aeneid is thus associated in his mind with opposition to the Church, and to his parents, as the noises of the mating, pagan yellowhammers are in conflict with the Church's bell ('Church is over, and its bell / Frightens the yellowhammers'). But the Aeneid also offers the old man vicarious heroic life, and effects a series of translations and metamorphoses in his mind: he becomes both Aeneas and Pallas; the yellowhammers become the bird-priests; a family sword, Dido's sword; the sun's colours, the blue and scarlet of the Roman soldiers' tunics, and the purple and gold of the funeral pall; the Trojan War, the American Civil War; the funeral of Pallas, that of the old man's Uncle Charles in his boyhood, and his own funeral to come—all merge in the strange, harsh circularities of dream.

Plainly, Lowell and the protagonist of his poem have much in common: the old man forgetting to go to Sunday service is

52. *P.*, p. 87.
53. *M.K.*, p. 3.

Lowell turning his back on New England's religious traditions, yet compelled in his poetry to register his admiration for a past he is cut off from, and the old man recalling his Uncle Charles is Lowell meeting the ancestor he would like to have met more than any other, Charles Russell Lowell. The old man enhances his unheroic life by turning his admiration into dream, and by kissing Pallas, 'lip to lip', witnesses the power of speech and poetry to transmit traditions; Lowell turns his admiration into myth and poetry. Yet, the last lines of the poem record an irrevocable discontinuity:

> It is I, I hold
> His sword to keep from falling, for the dust
> On the stuffed birds is breathless, for the bust
> Of young Augustus weighs on Vergil's shelf:
> It scowls into my glasses at itself.[54]

'Mother Marie Therese', which Randall Jarrell, with some justification, once called 'the best poem Mr Lowell has ever written',[55] is another poem about a rich past, and extends the book's secular trend in the story of a worldly, dionysiac nun— the Mother of the title—who indulged in such pagan pursuits as politics, reading Rabelais, and hunting. Her story is unravelled in the reminiscences of an old nun, who, like the old man in the previous poem with his dream of Pallas, suffers the frozen ambience of an unfulfilled present, and only comes to life at the thought of the departed Mother, whose life was only partly dedicated to the Church. The poem is part-satire of Mother Marie's lack of religious consistency; but primarily, it is an acknowledgement of her capacity to live in others. A Persephone torn between two worlds—in her case, secular and religious— her human qualities are finally more important than her religious ones, and part of the attraction of her story for Lowell must have been in her rebellion against religious orthodoxy—here humorously deflated in the figure of Father Turbot who, with unconscious irony, 'squeaked and stuttered: "N-n-nothing is so d-dead / As a dead s-s-sister"'. The humour, the playfulness, the colloquial vigour of the portrayals of Mother Marie, her

54. *P.*, p. 84.
55. Review of *The Mills of the Kavanaughs*, reprinted in *London and Boyers*, p. 39.

recorder, and **Father Turbot**—genuinely dramatic characters—recall both Chaucer and Browning, and the poem bubbles with worldly life, humanity and sympathy. If this is the only poem in the book to achieve unqualified success at a simple narrative level, it is probably because of its varied tones, its clear lines, and its firm narrative sweep, in which the couplets scud along in a way unique not only to this book, but to Lowell's output as a whole. Finally, there is the moving evocation of a wintry New Brunswick scene, in lines drenched in a cold imagery of the sea which mirrors the bare, fossilised world of the nuns' present lives:

> The dead, the sea's dead, has her sorrows, hours
> On end to lie tossing to the east, cold,
> Without bed-fellows, washed and bored and old,
> Bilged by her thoughts, and worked on by the worms,
> Until her fossil convent come to terms
> With the Atlantic.[56]

The most extensive treatment of many of the book's themes—madness, decayed traditions, family quarrels, suicide, death of love in marriage—is the title-poem, a poem in four parts and 16-line sections (which may owe something to Meredith's 'Modern Love' sequence), and, with more than 600 lines, by far the longest poem Lowell has written. The poem opens with Anne Kavanaugh sitting alone in the garden of the Kavanaugh family house and near the grave of her husband, Harry, and playing solitaire and reflecting on her marriage and on the decline of the family fortunes. A once-wealthy Catholic Maine family, the Kavanaughs have for a motto: 'Cut down, we flourish'. The motto is ironically inappropriate, but is translated into mythical terms via a statue of Persephone in the garden: in the poem, Anne Kavanaugh's marriage to Harry is the equivalent of Persephone's to Hades. Born into a poor family, and adopted by Harry's mother, her marriage to the heir of the Kavanaugh family had been a social ascent, but a descent into death also, in which she lacks any Persephone-like capacity to renew either the earth, the family fortunes, cure her husband's madness, or achieve the fruition of the love and sexual desire

56. *P.*, p. 89.

she had brought into her marriage. A naval officer retired after Pearl Harbour as a consequence of a mental instability brought about by causes which Lowell does not make clear, Henry had taken the road of insanity and suicide. The Kavanaugh family declined between the two World Wars—and thus suffered the fate of many old-established American families; but Lowell suggests that the decline is some sort of retribution for an earlier scion's—the ironically-named Red Kavanaugh—killing of Indians:

> who burned and buried child
> And squaw and elder in their river bed.[57]

Recalling 'At the Indian Killer's Grave', the passage is one more piece of evidence to suggest that the whole poem is, for Lowell, a dramatised version of his own family's fortunes: after all, his own father (like Harry Kavanaugh) declined after leaving the navy. It is probably this nearness to Lowell's own personal concerns that accounts for the difficulties experienced by the reader, and the uncertainties of Lowell in its composition. Though it is given a narrative framework by following the four 'seasons' of Anne's life—childhood, courtship, marriage and post-marriage—the poem, as a whole, drags its feet, with a minimum of variations of pace and tone, and lacking, for long stretches, either verbal excitement or character- and psychological-interest. Often, it is difficult to draw the line between exterior and interior reality: which are real sense impressions, and which imagined? With a poem of this length, it is essential that the reader should have *some* clear bearings, and the use of classical myths partly obfuscates the issue. Though Ovid's 'Metamorphoses' plays a similar role to Vergil's poem in 'Falling Asleep over the Aeneid', and, as in the latter poem, the Bible is in some sense an enemy, the basic Persephone-Hades myth is complicated by the intrusion of others from Ovid—principally the Echo-Narcissus myth—in an attempt by Lowell to suggest the complexity and ambiguity of Anne's relationship to her husband and to the world: she is partly in love with death, partly with herself. But one thing

57. *M.K.*, p. 10.

about the poem is permanently-powerful: the use of a marble-clear psychological scenery:

> She pushes on an oar.
> Her metal boat is moving from the shore.
>
> The heron warps its neck, a broken pick,
> To study its reflection on the scales,
> Or knife-bright shards of water lilies, quick
> In the dead autumn water with their snails
> And water lice.[58]

Many reviewers saw a saddening decline in the quality and range of Lowell's poetry with *The Mills of the Kavanaughs*, and the long silence after its publication seemed to substantiate their findings. Yet, whatever the individual qualities of the seven poems, they are an urgent attempt at the creation of a new kind of poetic tension—not one formed of partisanship and judgement, but in the fires of a mix of 'imitation', dramatic monologue, and personal sub-theme. Lowell is now exposing the horror and violence in the psyche, rather than in the State, Capitalism, and Calvinism, and that gulf between nature and supernature, and man's division from God, which was his starting-point, is explored at the level of character and plot. Finally, the book convinces as a sequence, a collection of poems on related themes. *The Mills of the Kavanaughs* is to shape strongly the whole of Lowell's subsequent career.

58. *M.K.*, p. 19.

3   The Flux of Experience

It is difficult now to re-capture the astonishing impact of *Life Studies* on its appearance in 1959. After a silence of something like eight years, Lowell seemed to have severed various ties with the past and launched out in a totally new direction. Briefly, he had made a final break with the 'symbol-ridden', allusive and rhetorical manner of his 'forties verse, having since confessed that he found its 'stiff, humourless and even impenetrable surface'[1] increasingly unacceptable; but he had also moved beyond the narrative-cum-dramatic mode of *The Mills of the Kavanaughs*, though it persists in 'The Banker's Daughter', 'A Mad Negro Soldier Confined at Munich', and ' "To Speak of the Woe that is in Marriage" ' in the new book. In retrospect, *Life Studies* appears as important for Lowell's development as *Responsibilities* had been for Yeats': he had found a characteristic voice, one which was to have a seminal effect on poetry in the late 'fifties and 'sixties. Like Wordsworth, Hopkins, Yeats and Eliot before him, he had appropriated for his generation a real world of simple textures, and embodied it in a language nearer to a prose and colloquial norm than existing poetic practice allowed for.

The book's title inevitably suggests a poetic equivalent of studies from the life in painting, and one critic has called the new poems 'dry-point etchings'.[2] After the rhetoric of the first three books, one senses in the general lowering of the poetic temperature that Lowell has freed himself from the influence of Tate. It was inevitable, for Tate stood for an aristocratic conception of poetry; it surfaced in his introduction to *Land of Unlikeness*, where he contrasted Lowell with 'the democratic poets who enthusiastically greet the advent of the slave-society'.[3]

1. *Ostroff*, p. 108.   2. *Staples*, p. 66.   3. *London and Boyers*, p. 2.

43

Lowell's change of style with *Life Studies* went with a less lofty, more engaged response than Tate's to the manifestations of a master-slave mentality in contemporary American life. After three years in Europe, he had returned to settle in Boston in 1954 at the height of the Cold War and the years of conformity and stagnation symbolised by the names of Senator McCarthy and President Eisenhower; and the suggestions of a petrifaction in the national life are everywhere in *Life Studies*. The new influence to replace Tate's was that of Elizabeth Bishop, to whom Lowell was to dedicate both his next book, *Imitations*, and the last and most celebrated poem of *Life Studies*, 'Skunk Hour'. In a conversation with Stanley Kunitz, Lowell referred to her as 'a sort of bridge between Tate's formalism and Williams' informal art'.[4] A poet of landscape, the particular strength of Elizabeth Bishop's early poetry is in the accurate arrangement of detail; if Williams can be said, in Lowell's words to 'enter America', she charts it. Obviously, she encouraged Lowell in his search for a metonymic use of detail, in his effort to see man in terms of landscape ('Man changed to landscape'[5]), and in keeping extraneous comment down to as little as possible. In her later work, as in *Questions of Travel*,[6] she uses details and landscape in the kind of alive, intense and disturbing way that anticipates Lowell's own achievement in his *Life Studies*. Of her work, Lowell has said: 'She's gotten a world, not just a way of writing. She seldom writes a poem that doesn't have that exploratory quality; yet it's very firm, it's not like beat poetry, it's all controlled':[7] these words could be used of the best of the *Life Studies* poems.

The other important influence was that of prose. In the early 'fifties, some sort of exploration of the possibilities of prose seemed to Lowell the appropriate way out for him from the impasse his poetry found itself in; increasingly, he felt 'that the best style for poetry was none of the many poetic styles in English, but something like the prose of Chekhov or Flaubert'.[8] The most

4. Stanley Kunitz, '*Talk with Robert Lowell*', in *The New York Times Book Review*, 4 October 1964, pp. 34–9.
5. *L.S.*, p. 11.
6. *Questions of Travel*, New York (Farrar, Straus & Giroux) 1965.
7. *P.R.*, p. 248.   8. *Ostroff*, p. 108.

successful poem in the early part of the *Life Studies* sequence—
'My Last Afternoon with Uncle Devereux Winslow'—began as
prose,[9] and at the heart of the book is '91 Revere Street', which
owes something to the prose of Flaubert, Turgenev and Chekhov.

The experience of writing '91 Revere Street' must have been
crucial to the making of *Life Studies*. It is a disturbing, bizarre
comedy of a house and its inheritance: a house which is both a
microcosm of a certain strata of the Boston upper-class world
and, with its class and racial stresses, the story of the United
States. Consisting of forty-odd pages of fragmentary reminiscence,
it offers a series of weird family portraits, descriptions of parts
of the house, and cameos of events as viewed from the double
perspective of Lowell as child and as adult. In a society obsessed
by concerns of class, status and possessions, the house itself and
its furniture provide as much information as we need about
the failures, isolation, and psychic hungers of the characters
and their unheroic lives. Thus, Lowell refers twice to the family
dustbins:

> Father believed that churchgoing was undignified for a
> naval man; his Sunday mornings were given to useful
> acts such as lettering his three new galvanized garbage
> cans: R. T. S. Lowell—U.S.N.

> Out in the alley the sun shone irreverently on our
> three garbage cans lettered: R. T. S. Lowell—U.S.N.

In this secular milieu, religion takes second place to useful acts
about the house. This apparently insignificant pair of references
takes a sombre resonance in retrospect—from 'Memories of West
Street and Lepke' and 'Skunk Hour', where other dustbins are
properties in a world of animal scavenging and brute survival,
and from a later book's 'Waking Early Sunday Morning', where
the universal American of the poem devotes his Sundays to the
same trivial round as Lowell's father.

Lowell has a superb ear and eye for the absurd: the father

9. *Conversations on the Craft of Poetry*, ed. Cleanth Brooks and Robert Penn
Warren, New York (Holt, Rinehart & Winston) 1961, p. 41. But other poems,
according to the *Paris Review* interview, 'were started in strict metre', p. 246.

45

sleeping every night at the naval yard, Great Aunt Sarah practising on a dummy piano for a concert she never gives, the father metamorphosed by the mother into a Siegfried, vino rosso in teacups, a loudspeaker in the shape of a sombrero, a tea-kettle barometer. He is also very good at speech, and captures well the between-the-Wars slang, and the idiom of bluff navy men. The prose is at times more than a little mannered, with its naggingly-predictable oxymoronic phrases[10] ('her uniqueness and normality'; 'a buoyant tranquillity'; 'Father's submissive tenacity'), which Lowell uses to convey the ambivalences of these Lowell and Winslow lives. But '91 Revere Street' is a fine piece of social history of America in the 'twenties and 'thirties, the Depression Years. It is also a saga of survival; the mother uses the latter word about her son in an unconsciously prophetic way: 'Oh Bob, if you are going to resign, do it *now* so I can at least plan for your son's *survival* and education on a single continent.'

'91 Revere Street' had been a long time in gestation. In spite of the cosmic themes of *Land of Unlikeness* and *Lord Weary's Castle*, its roots, and the first inklings of the *Life Studies* style, are in poems such as 'Between the Porch and the Altar', 'Winter in Dunbarton', 'Her Dead Brother', 'The First Sunday in Lent', 'In the Cage', 'In Memory of Arthur Winslow', and in particular, 'Mary Winslow' and 'Buttercups':

> When we were children our papas were stout
> And colourless as seaweed or the floats
> At anchor off New Bedford. We were shut
> In gardens where our brassy sailor coats
> Made us like black-eyed susans bending out
> Into the ocean. Then my teeth were cut:
> A levelled broom-pole butt

10. For Lowell, oxymorons are a shorthand way of conveying conflict and ambiguity. There is a particularly large number of them in 'Randall Jarrell 1914–1965: An Appreciation', reprinted in *Randall Jarrell 1914–1965*, ed. Lowell, Peter Taylor and Robert Penn Warren, New York (Farrar, Straus & Giroux) 1967, p. 101–17: 'murderous intuitive phrases', 'the same hesitating satire and sympathy', 'monstrously knowing and monstrously innocent', 'beings that are determined, passive and sacrificial'. Lowell is particularly fond of matings of the decorous and the disturbing.

> Was pushed into my thin
> And up-turned chin.[11]

('Buttercups')

These last two poems of family reminiscence—about defeat, the omnipresence of death, innocence, precarious dignity, the pains of growing up—anticipate *Life Studies*' delicate use of simple vowel and consonantal effects: for example, in the line 'Grips at the poised relations sipping sherry' in 'Mary Winslow'. If they differ from the *Life Studies* family portraits, it is in their formal cadences, less colloquial bent, and in the way Lowell more determinedly forces them in the direction of symbol, allusion and comment.

But this is not to suggest there is anything haphazard or casual about the construction of the *Life Studies* poems. The colloquial, homely and photographic surface has an air of understatement, but only in order to allow the details to stand out with particular force; the voice of the poems is often the 'calm, sometimes even placid, speaking voice'[12] one critic refers to, but at other times, it has the turbulent edge of desperation, with emotion frequently breaking the reticent, controlled surface:

> Father's death was abrupt and unprotesting.
> His vision was still twenty-twenty.[13]
>
> ... sky-blue tracks of the commuters' railroad shone
> like a double-barrelled shotgun
> through the scarlet late August sumac,
> multiplying like cancer. . . .[14]

These are studies of particular lives in a particular time and place; family history now provides metaphors for poetry, and the metaphysical and mythical Boston of Lowell's early poetry has become an historical Boston in decline. And there is a sharp poignancy in the book's title: so many of the poems are about death, and overshadowed by the family graveyard.

Two poems about the Winslow grandparents illustrate the

11. *P.*, p. 28. 12. *Staples*, p. 66.
13. *L.S.*, p. 88. 14. *L.S.*, p. 87.

new manner well—'Dunbarton' and 'Grandparents'. It is instructive to read them with the earlier 'In Memory of Arthur Winslow' in mind. The sense of worldly, possession-dominated, money-making lives is still present—

> Grandmother, like a Mohammedan, still wears her thick
> lavendar mourning and touring veil,
> the Pierce Arrow clears its throat in a horse-stall.
> Then the dry road dust rises to whiten
> the fatigued elm leaves—
> the nineteenth century, tired of children, is gone
> ('Grandparents')[15]

—and yet the details draw back at the edge of some symbolic import; the last line's self-regarding allusiveness defuses the poem at the point where it might have become too portentous. Though these two poems are about the spiritual vacuity of present and past lives, the details hold us in a bond of nostalgia and affection at some irredeemable loss. Our attention is drawn to oddities— the grandmother 'like a Mohammedan'; a car in a horse stall— and in this way, each figure is rescued from some safe, remote corner of history, and revivified, like the objects which sustain the poems' fabric: the greenwood stove *chatters*, the Pierce Arrow *clears its throat*, as in other *Life Studies* poems, an electric-razor *purrs*, wheels have *a querulous hush-hush*, furniture has *a tiptoe air*. Suggestions of utter stillness—

> His favourite ball, the number three,
> still hides the coffee stain[16]

> the clump of virgin pine still stretched patchy ostrich
> necks
> over the disused millpond's fragrantly woodstained
> water[17]

—are unambiguously joined to hints of some final staining and decay. But one also detects in the excess of modifiers in the last

15. *L.S.*, p. 82.   16. *L.S.*, p. 82.   17. *L.S.*, p. 79.

line quoted both a loathness to let go, and a concern to pin down precisely.

Life Studies is in four parts, with the book's title also the title of the fourth part, which is the climax of the whole proceedings. Excluding 'Beyond the Alps', which is uniquely caught between two poetic worlds, and the prose '91 Revere Street', there are four types of poems: childhood and family reminiscences; tributes to writers; dramatic third-person narratives; and directly personal poems about Lowell's various predicaments. More than any of Lowell's books, it is carefully shaped, and moves in one overall direction: from a general account of civilisation ('Beyond the Alps') to one man's personal agonies ('Skunk Hour'), from a journey across the centuries, to the events of an hour. Part Two of the book—'91 Revere Street'—was omitted from the earlier English editions, but restored later, as a token that, without it, the book loses the added conviction which comes from constant illuminating cross-references between prose and poems; for example, in 'Commander Lowell', we are told that the mother's voice is 'electric / with a hysterical, unmarried panic'—'91 Revere Street' offers several examples of the voice in action.[18] The poems tend to overlap; themes and motifs are announced, discarded, and then taken up later. To mention only one example, there is the motif of grandparents; in 'Beyond the Alps', we have a picture of self-confident Victorian grandparents; then we come nearer home, with several pictures of Lowell's grandparents, and the refuge and consolation they represented for the young Lowell in retreat from his immediate parents—so much of *Life Studies* is about surrogate parents. Near the end of the book, Lowell reflects that he has a daughter 'young enough to be my granddaughter'. Simple objects also recur and take on the force of symbols: for example, cars, beds and razors.

Part One consists of four poems with a common theme of breakdown and disintegration. Located in four different periods of history (three of them are precisely dated), they offer a general setting for what follows in the rest of the book: all history in *Life Studies* telescopes down to the isolated hero of 'Skunk Hour' at the end. 'Beyond the Alps', the opening poem, takes its title

18. See Chapter One, p. 6.

from a line in 'Falling Asleep Over the Aeneid'. Very much a coda to Lowell's early career, it is at one level clearly about his abandonment of Roman Catholicism,[19] though he claims to have left the Church some while before writing the poem. A sequence of four sonnets in the final version, it has much of that pull of a bludgeoning, dense manner against a strict formal control of Lowell's early poetry; and yet the rhymes fall haphazardly. It is a record of both a physical journey[20] in 1950 (the year 'when Pius XII defined the dogma of Mary's bodily assumption' and the failure of a Swiss expedition to Everest) and Lowell's spiritual journey from Augustine's City of God, of Mussolini, Caesar, and Pope, to Paris, city of the human dimension, of Art, the secular 'black classic', the post-Fall Baudelairean city. 'Man/life changed to landscape' is the poem's key phrase: man's spiritual situation and progress is seen in terms of landscape, which is the method of the family poems, and points to the role of the Nautilius Island scene of 'Skunk Hour'. But the geographical journey is paralleled by an historical journey. In their rise and fall, civilisations repeat the same mistakes, and Pope, Caesar and Mussolini are placed on the same level of Roman moral depravity, endlessly circling the same round of deceptions: Mussolini unfurls the eagle of Caesar; the Duce's 'Lynched, bare, booted skull' answers to the same intention to deceive as Saint Peter's 'brazen sandal'. Compared to these, our Victorian capitalist ancestors are a kind of honesty personified:

> I envy the conspicuous
> waste of our grandparents on their grand tours—
> long-haired Victorian sages accepted the universe,
> while breezing on their trust funds through the world.[21]

This workaday secularism is preferable to the calculatedly disguised secularism of the Church and State: in a world of modern rationalism, mystery devolves into hypocrisy:

19. For Jerome Mazzaro, (*The Poetic Themes of Robert Lowell*, p. 119,) the whole of *Life Studies* signals 'the loss of the Christian experience'.

20. In 'Between the Porch and the Altar', the protagonist reflects: 'The past / Is cities from a train'. *P*., p. 55.

21. *L.S.*, p. 11.

When the Vatican made Mary's Assumption dogma,
the crowds at San Pietro screamed *Papa*.
The Holy Father dropped his shaving glass, . . .
his pet canary chirped on his left hand.
The lights of science couldn't hold a candle
to Mary risen—at one miraculous stroke,
angel-wing'd, gorgeous as a jungle bird![22]

Outrageous puns and vulgar clichés are made to witness the
world's capitulation to 'the monstrous human crush', and imagery,
symbols, and form work together to convey that mixture of order
and disorder characteristic of civilisations. Thus, mountains in
the poem represent human aspiration in art, philosophy and
religion, that desire to impose order on experience which is
reflected in the poem's outer order of the sonnet form; but the
human reality is different—the history of violence in Pope,
Caesar and Mussolini—and this is reflected in the inner violence
of the poem: 'mind and murder' are thus bedfellows. Society is
seen to depend on something animal and instinctive, though it
pretends otherwise; and thus the poem goes part of the way to
establishing a context for these things in the later poems of *Life
Studies*. More than a personal account of a loss of faith, the poem
is a savage descant on the inability of civilisations to escape a
round of violence and deceit, and Lowell's almost psychopathic
despair and disillusion at the world's abuse of power matches in
its cynicism passages of Pound's *Cantos*. But ultimately, 'Beyond
the Alps' is a sane plea for accepting the impurity of experience
as the only reality—life lived 'beyond the Alps'—a bitter facing
of an irredeemably prosaic world. Given the kind of things the
poem is saying, it is pointless to protest as some critics have done
that, on leaving the Church, Lowell offers no more detailed
examination of doctrine than he gave on entering it; or that he
doesn't make it clear whether he is principally attacking the
Church for its dogmas, or humanity for its failure to live up to
them. The rest of *Life Studies* develops from the agnostic, existentialist position Lowell has reached in this poem, and arcs from
the break-up of Paris announced here to Lowell's own break-
downs in the book's final poems.

22. *L.S.*, p. 11.

The first nine poems of the 'Life Studies' sequence proper—from 'My Last Afternoon with Uncle Devereux Winslow' to 'During Fever'—are about Lowell's grandparents, uncles and aunts, and parents; but we move nearer to the adult Lowell with each poem. The themes of the sequence are: the generations; conformity and rebellion; failure; social snobbery; the world of possessions. 'My Last Afternoon with Uncle Devereux Winslow' is perhaps the finest of the several elegies that Lowell has written about members of the Winslow side of the family.[23] It is part Mutability Ode, part a Vanity of Human Wishes. In four sections, it shows the effect on the young Lowell of the early death of a young uncle; but it is also an attempt to see life and death as process, to fit the rebellions and conformities of the Winslows and Lowells, and of the poet himself, to a cycle of death and renewal. Surrounded by images of death and decay, the young Lowell searches for life: in an idealisation of his grandparents, daydreams, and in an effort towards an 'Olympian poise', something imperishable with which to confront the mechanical, dead life of possessions—

> *Tockytock, tockytock*
> clumped our Alpine, Edwardian cuckoo clock,
> slung with strangled, wooden game[24]

—and death in the natural world. The poem brings out what is only implied in '91 Revere Street': this is the 'sunset hour' of a family—

> It was the sunset on Sadie and Nellie
> bearing pitchers of ice-tea, . . .[25]

> lurid in the doldrums of the sunset hour,
> my Great Aunt Sarah
> was learning *Samson and Delilah*[26]

23. There is an interesting survey of Lowell's Winslow poems by Marjorie Perloff: 'Death by Water: The Winslow Elegies of Robert Lowell', in *English Literary History*, XXXIV, 1967, pp. 116–40.

24. *L.S.*, p. 73.   25. *L.S.*, p. 74.   26. *L.S.*, p. 75.

—beached high and dry in a post-war world and unsustained by an earlier age's simpler pieties. Only after the context is established is the death of the uncle introduced—in the last section of the poem. The delayed entrance is essential; the uncle's death offers no consolation, no suggestion of a fulfilment. It merely takes its due place in an universal cycle:

> Come Winter,
> Uncle Devereux would blend to the one colour.[27]

> Uncle Devereux was closing camp for the winter.[28]

The young Lowell receives disturbing intimations of a seasonal and elemental process.

'My Last Afternoon' was a key poem in Lowell's development. It shows a brilliant use of material from '91 Revere Street': thus, we have a sharply-pointed description of the Great Aunt Sarah already met, whose neurotic, aimless life is made to relate to both the young Lowell's, and his parents', daydreams. It has a careful pattern of imagery, varying tones, shifting perspectives (for example, we see Uncle Devereux largely through the grandfather's eyes); there is a great resilience and economy, and constantly changing speeds. An art of juxtaposition basically, it can encompass bare statement very effectively. Here is a superb mixture of statement, comment and metaphor near the end of the poem:

> Uncle Devereux stood behind me.
> He was as brushed as Bayard, our riding horse.
> His face was putty.
> His blue coat and white trousers
> grew sharper and straighter.
> His coat was a blue jay's tail,
> his trousers were solid cream from the top of the bottle.
> He was animated, hierarchical,
> like a ginger snap man in a clothes-press.
> He was dying of the incurable Hodgkin's disease. . . .[29]

27. *L.S.*, p. 78.   28. *L.S.*, p. 76.   29. *L.S.*, pp. 77–8.

The details invest the figure of Uncle Devereux with a kind of excess animation, that of a great portrait-painting. So that we get both the reality, the child's view of things in the comparisons involving the blue jay's tail, the cream, and the ginger snap man, and the adult's, which sees in Uncle Devereux a hierarchy which devolves down to him. The lines seem to generate their own inner tension, rather than receive it from outside; whatever pattern there is in the Winslow lives is left to find itself.

The remaining poems of the first part of the 'Life Studies' sequence are not all at the same high level as 'My Last Afternoon', a poem which creates a whole Chekhovian miniature world. Sometimes documentation substitutes for art; in other places, the manner digresses into whimsy, or a distendedness and laxity of style, as if Lowell is over-indulging in a new-found stylistic freedom. Sometimes, the 'stabbing detail' doesn't generate the 'universal',[30] and the essential comment on human behaviour refuses to come out of the particular situation. On these occasions, we are just a little too aware of the poet's aristocratic airs:[31] the lines are too fastidious and nit-picking.

The final achievement of the new style comes with the personal poems, from 'Waking in the Blue' to the end of the book: the best of Lowell in *Life Studies* is in the poetry that charts his own survival—and this is going to be just as true of subsequent books. These later poems are exploratory, dramatic, and ambivalent. Whereas the early *Life Studies* poetry is a poetry of juxtaposed scenes, conversations, and impressions, here plot re-emerges —in the sense of a carefully worked-out narrative sequence; and the new firmness of line argues a dramatic progression from the prescriptive forms of the 'forties poetry towards a truly organic form. But most importantly, the poet-protagonist has moved to the centre of the stage: the culture of the self created by the rest of the book produces its hero, and we see what the previous poems have been leading up to.

Now, Lowell and 'the mad negro' of an earlier poem,[32] with

30. 'William Carlos Williams', in *Hudson Review*, XIV, 1961–62, p. 531.

31. Joseph Bennett is scathing about this 'collection of lazily recollected and somewhat snobbish memoirs', in 'Two Americans, a Brahmin and the Bourgeoisie', in *Hudson Review*, XII, 1959, pp. 431–9.

32. *L.S.*, p. 16.

his isolation, anguish, madness, and struggle to preserve identity amidst disintegration, merge. Exhibiting many of the characteristics of European poetry since Baudelaire[33]—a baring of the anguished soul and an unremitting self-examination—these poems are obviously 'confessional', but the word hardly does justice to the taut structures, the complex range of attitudes, and the finely-honed language, which can startle us with contemporary clichés or inject a heightened poetic image to moving effect, and the wit and detachment that can present the poet in various poses: self-ironic, self-exposing, self-analytical. Thus, in 'Waking in the Blue', Lowell's picture of a period spent by him in a mental home achieves its horrified edge partly from the detachment with which Lowell can view himself—a leading intellectual and member of a distinguished Boston family, searching like the attendant for 'the meaning of meaning' in a select asylum amongst 'thoroughbred mental cases'—from the mixture of pity and wry humour ('what use is my sense of humour?') with which he describes his fellow inmates, and from the way in which he sees himself as somehow in the grasp of the objects of his miniature world:

> After a hearty New England breakfast,
> I weigh two hundred pounds
> this morning. Cock of the walk,
> I strut in my turtle-necked French sailor's jersey
> before the metal shaving mirrors,
> and see the shaky future grow familiar
> in the pinched, indigenous faces
> of these thoroughbred mental cases,
> twice my age and half my weight.[34]

In these last poems, there are frequent windings and unwindings of threads that connect past and present; 'Memories of West Street and Lepke' does this superbly. In another of *Life Studies*' several portrayals of a controlled life, a middle-aged

33. Lowell has often been pictured as a modern American Baudelaire. For lengthy discussions of this topic, see Irvin Ehrenpreis, 'The Age of Lowell', in *American Poetry*, ed. Ehrenpreis, London (Edward Arnold) 1965, pp. 94–5; and Steven Axelrod, 'Baudelaire and the Poetry of Robert Lowell', in *Twentieth Century Literature*, XVII, 1971, pp. 257–74.   34. *L.S.*, p. 96.

Lowell simultaneously looks back on his time in prison as a wartime conscientious objector, and at his conformist present:

> These are the tranquillized *Fifties*,
> and I am forty. Ought I to regret my seedtime?
> I was a fire-breathing Catholic C.O.,
> and made my manic statement, . . .[35]

His present ritualised and pointless life has disturbing echoes of his father's compromise with his former ambitions: has he, like his father, lost 'the ability to explode'? The reference to the 'young Republican' reminds us that these are the Eisenhower Cold War years, and Lowell's feeling of personal inertia is matched nationally. The only suggestion of new life, new possibilities, is in his daughter, Harriet, who rises 'Like the sun . . . in her flame-flamingo infants' wear'; but even this consolation is muted by the reflection that she is young enough to be his granddaughter. In pondering on his prison experiences in the 'forties, Lowell measures his 'manic statement' against those of other prison inmates—in particular, those of Abramowitz, a pacifist, and the very different Czar Lepke, a hired murderer. Abramowitz is a 'flyweight' pacifist (like Thoreau, perhaps?), without Lowell's belligerency, but even so, his pacificism brings down on his own head the violence he abhors. Lowell is reiterating the point that he has often returned to in his poetry—that 'violence and idealism have some occult connection';[36] and the poem is a probing of the connection within himself. It comes to the fore in his picture of Czar Lepke; in spite of his brutal past, the man is an image of total withdrawal:

> Flabby, bald, lobotomized,
> he drifted in a sheepish calm,
> where no agonising reappraisal
> jarred his concentration on the electric chair—
> hanging like an oasis in his air
> of lost connections . . .[37]

Lowell throws up the possibility that his own present half-suspended state is a version of Lepke's lobotomised violence.

35. *L.S.*, p. 99.   36. *Alvarez*, p. 41.   37. *L.S.*, p. 100.

But the details also suggest that Lepke is a version of the state of the nation in the 1950's: his cell is 'segregated', full of 'things forbidden the common man', including 'two toy American / flags'. This is a Lowell who both senses that 'everyone's tired of my turmoil', yet ill-at-ease with conformity, and is aware that the state holds a locked razor, administers shock-treatment to its citizens. In the strange figure of Lepke, Lowell has created an overwhelmingly-accurate focussing image for himself, his father, his family, the state—all 'hanging like an oasis in [an] air / of lost connections'.

Throughout *Life Studies*, Lowell follows the processes of disintegration in both the world and the self—empty traditions, stultifying conformity, meaningless rituals, war, imprisonment, madness, family quarrels, unfulfilled ambitions—so that, in a real sense, the journey announced in the first poem, 'Beyond the Alps', becomes a journey across both a modern Waste Land and a landscape of the mind. The culmination of these themes, and a most harrowing, yet triumphant exposition of them, is in the book's final poem, 'Skunk Hour', the most inwardly exploratory of all the *Life Studies* poems, truly a psychological drama. The poem has meant a great deal to Lowell,[38] both as a breakthrough to a new style (very different from, but related to, the style of 'My Last Afternoon'), and as a crucial stage in self-exploration; if any poem in *Life Studies* suggests the intensity of the struggle on both counts, it is this one.

In effect, the poem is in two parts, with the final two stanzas of the second part as the climax of the whole thing. The first four stanzas present a picture of a landscape at various times of the seasonal year; against this background, three odd, rootless inhabitants of a New England summer resort lead dead, purposeless and selfishly-isolated lives centred on a use, or misuse, of money. The terms used to describe them suggest three stages of American history, presented in an off-hand, broken way: a rural, religious past; an age of capitalist expansion; modern rootless tourism.[39] Their world's abuse of Time and Nature is summed up in 'The season's ill', and in perhaps the most pregnant line of the first part, 'A red fox stain covers Blue Hill'. The first

38. See his contribution to the symposium on the poem in *Ostroff*, pp. 107–10.
39. J. F. Nims says the poem is 'among other things, a study of the Puritan syndrome'. *Ibid.*, p. 91.

inhabitant—an 'hermit heiress' searching for privacy, and in her dotage—is an odd picture of futility: though she hankers after the hierarchical distinctions of the nineteenth century, she is superseded by her son and her tenant farmer. (It is interesting to note the many ways of life suggested in the two stanzas devoted to her: heiress; shepherdess (sheep); Spartan; bishop; selectman; hermit; farmer.) The next figure is also displaced by social inferiors: a millionaire whose boat is auctioned off to fishermen. The third figure, a homosexual decorator, sees marriage as the only answer to the problems of his ailing business. Throughout the first part, the suggestions are of ways of life gone to seed, a world of sterile sex, fading affluence, lost social orders, passing seasons, life turning into death, and of the intrusion of non-human into human life—an anticipation of the skunks of the second half. Each stanza is distinct from its neighbour, as if to emphasise the isolation of the people it describes.

The first part describes a general state of culture, but it is also, in a sense, a weird projection of the eccentric lives of the Lowell family we have already met, and of the disorientated lives of the inmates in 'Waking in the Blue'. After this orchestrated background, we have in the second part the agonised solo of the protagonist and the personal breakdown that he faces in the midst of the general breakdown—an ill-spirit abroad in an ill-season. The poem moves into a landscape with suggestions of St. John of the Cross' 'dark night of the soul', though Lowell himself has suggested a more secular night:[40]

> One dark night,
> my Tudor Ford climbed the hill's skull,
> I watched for love-cars. Lights turned down,
> they lay together, hull to hull,
> where the graveyard shelves on the town. . . .
> my mind's not right.[41]

This prowler peeping on lovers is a projection of the loveless inhabitants of Nautilius Island in the first half. In these lines

40. 'My night is not gracious, but secular, puritan, and agnostical. An Existentialist night. Somewhere in my mind was a passage from Sartre or Camus about reaching some point of final darkness where the one free act is suicide.' *Ibid.*, p. 107.　　　41. *L.S.*, p. 104.

here is the kind of basic detail which shows how valuable '91 Revere Street' is to a full appreciation of *Life Studies*: Lowell's father measured his status in a constant progression of bigger and better cars, but this protagonist's Tudor (two-door) Ford shows the rock-bottom at which he operates.

In the next stanza, there is a harrowing picture of loneliness and thoughts of suicide, where the extraneous hells of Lowell's forties verse have been replaced by the self-generated inner hells of the human spirit:

> A car radio bleats,
> 'Love, O careless Love . . .' I hear
> my ill-spirit sob in each blood cell,
> as if my hand were at its throat . . .
> I myself am hell,
> nobody's here.[42]

This Satan/Hamlet/voyeur of the poem trembles on the edge of an abyss of total disintegration. All the literary references in 'Skunk Hour' relate to world-weariness and spiritual torment—and there is a 'buried' reference to the Crucifixion; but the stress is also on the universality of the situation described, and because of this, we can move at the end into a harmony of a minimal kind, a dying into life, which is perhaps the effect of the greatest tragedies. But before this point, there is the entry of the skunks in a search for food—something more natural than the 'thirsting' of the heiress for privacy. Paradoxically, they represent a rich life, as opposed to the earlier inhabitants' dead lives, a kind of basic passion, animality and wildness which contrasts markedly with the tameness and conformity Lowell surveys in other *Life Studies* poems, and to the 'dotage' of the heiress and the Church's dry life in this poem:

> They march on their soles up Main Street: . . .
> under the chalk-dry and spar spire
> of the Trinitarian Church.[43]

42. *L.S.*, p. 104.

43. *L.S.*, p. 104. Interestingly, in John Updike's *The Centaur*, 1963, p. 262 of Penguin edition, the hero, George, says, 'All Nature means to me is garbage and confusion and the stink of skunk—brroo!'

Life Studies began with the rejection of a Church surrounded by rituals and pomp, and it ends with the rejection of a very different one; both are rejected in favour of basic life. In the same way, the mother-skunk is a vivid contrast to the mother-of-a-bishop heiress of the opening, and in her kittens, there is a possibility of a new life similar to that Lowell found in his baby daughter, with her 'flame-flamingo infants' wear'.

In their purposeful progression to the dustbins, the skunks offer the protagonist, who has been searching for love and meaning, an emblem of generation, so that the last stanza's first and last lines mark a minimal triumph, a supplanting of *Life Studies'* failed heroes—from history, the Lowell family, other writers—by the poet as hero: 'I stand on top . . . and will not scare': the contrast is with the mountains of 'Beyond the Alps', and with the Golgotha/Calvary of this poem. So a low point of despair has led, as Lowell puts it, to an 'ambiguous affirmation'.[44]

There is a quality of direct self-realisation here that makes the poem a suitable climax to *Life Studies*—which is not to say that Lowell has abandoned art for direct confession:

> 'Skunk Hour' was written backwards, first the last
> two stanzas, I think, and then the next to the last
> two. Anyway, there was a time when I had the last
> four stanzas much as they now are and nothing before
> them. I found the bleak personal violence repellent.
> All was too close, though watching the lovers was not
> mine, but from an anecdote about Walt Whitman in
> his old age. I began to feel that real poetry came, not
> from fierce confessions, but from something almost
> meaningless but imagined; I was haunted by an
> image of a blue china doorknob. I never used the
> doorknob, or knew what it meant (Lowell uses white
> ones in 'Waking Early Sunday Morning'!), yet some-
> how it started the current of images in my opening
> stanzas. They were written in reverse order, and at
> last gave my poem an earth to stand on, and space to
> breathe.[45]

44. *Ostroff*, p. 107.
45. *Op. cit.*, pp. 109–10.

The poem is, in Eliot's words, an 'expression of *significant* emotion, emotion which has its life in the poem and not in the history of the poet'.[46] 'Skunk Hour' is the poem that all the other poems, and '91 Revere Street' have provided documentation for. Yet it also looks forward, in style and content, to the next book: its structure of short-lined sestets is a firm, shaping one similar to those in *For the Union Dead*. This disciplined form saves the self-revelations from an access of melodrama and sentimentality; another means is the pointed use of literary allusions—to Shakespeare, St. John of the Cross, and *Paradise Lost*. And most importantly, it achieves, more than any of the *Life Studies* poems, a wonderful sense of contexts—religious, family, social and literary.

Life Studies began with a poem about the world, and ends with a poem about the self. 'Beyond the Alps' set up the two poles of the book: Rome, standing for tradition, mind, authority, and the ice-like blockage of the poem about Eisenhower's inauguration, offers a minimal stasis or stability; Paris, representing individualism, freedom, imagination, and flux, exposes us to the darker reaches of the spirit. The whole book charts a personal zigzag journey between these two; yet is is also a general cultural journey through a decade. The 'fifties stagnation is strikingly caught in such words and phrases as 'loafing', 'dawdling', 'tamed', 'drugged', 'tranquillized', 'dotage', 'hardly passionate', and 'lost connections'; but behind their use is Lowell's persistent suggestion that the period's 'sheepish calm', allied to pressures towards conformity, hid some deep disturbance of a violent kind, as if an Eisenhower fronted a Czar Lepke. It is this context of social criticism that gives authority to the examination of the self in *Life Studies*, for the latter without the first would be considerably more neurotic, and less universal in its application; and behind all these poems, but particularly the last four, is an insistence that the individual psychological state is a reflection of society's general condition, contrary to the implicit denial of this in the 'forties verse. Hence, the force of 'Ought I to regret my seed-time?': Lowell is now acknowledging that his social stance of the 'forties was more ambiguously-motivated than the poetry of

46. 'Tradition and the Individual Talent', in *Selected Essays*, London (Faber) 1932, p. 22.

the time admitted to. But his particular agony in the 'fifties was that, though he needed himself to enter a period of tranquillisation in order to free himself from earlier misplaced energies, true freedom means to 'free-lance out along the razor's edge'.[47]

The gains of the *Life Studies* style are many: an affectionate, non-sardonic humour and wit; those warmer emotions of love, nostalgia, regret and pity that rarely appeared in the early poetry; and a controlled use of cliché and colloquial language that contrasts with the early poetry's often hollow rhetoric. In moving from life as allegory to man/life as landscape, Lowell has not always avoided self-indulgence, over-plangent pathos, and a false simplicity: parts of the family portraits hardly rise above the uncomplicated level of Edgar Lee Masters in such *Spoon River* poems as 'Lucius Atherton', 'Washington McNeeley' and 'Father Molloy',[48] with their portrayals of drab, broken-winged lives in a repressive small-town community, though Lowell's lines are nearly always individually more pointed. But the risks are part of the honesty of the proceedings; Lowell has left the Alps of his early work, and come down to earth. What is his final position? There seems an acceptance of basic and instinctive life, and the intimations of love in wife and child; but are reason, system of values, judgement, and art thrown into the melting-pot? It is, as Lowell says, an 'ambiguous affirmation'.

47. *L.S.*, p. 102.
48. *Spoon River Anthology*, London (T. Werner Laurie) 1915.

4   In Search of a Tradition

In the published account of John McCormick's interview with Lowell, there is an interesting passage where Lowell says: 'Every writer has to be a thief. He has to be *childishly* ambitious and even say to himself, like Racine, what would Sophocles think of this?'[1] After *Life Studies*, in which he had established an auto-biographical context for his poetry to work within, Lowell's ambitiousness took on more and more the character of this desire to measure his achievement against that of others. The result was a series of works based on 'originals' by other writers: namely, *Imitations* (1961); *Phaedra* (1961); *The Old Glory* (1965); and *Prometheus Bound* (1969). In all these, Lowell makes certain classics of European culture available to the contemporary reader; *The Old Glory* is really no exception, as the authors it works from—Hawthorne and Melville—are as much European classics as the others, and particularly close to a general modern literary sensibility.

Translation and adaptation have, of course, been very much in the air in the twentieth century, for in a time of general cultural breakdown, they are an important means available to the writer of retaining some personal cultural roots; but there is also an implicit acknowledgement in a lot of modern translation that, as Donald Davie puts it in *Purity of Diction in English Verse*, 'the best modern poems often read as if they were good translations from another language.'[2] At the heart of many modern discussions of poetic theory lie two almost contradictory beliefs: that 'poetry' inheres in the very untranslatable texture of the native, often idiomatic language, and that for this reason, a poem is an object unique and autonomous; that there is a

1. 'Falling Asleep over Grillparzer: An Interview with Robert Lowell', in *Poetry*, LXXXI, January 1953, p. 278.
2. *Purity of Diction in English Verse*, London (Routledge) 1967, pp. 10–11.

contemporary sensibility which at its strongest can overcome language, and even period, barriers. This particular issue has been raised for years by the work of Pound—both the Cantos and the 'translations'—and every modern translator works, to some extent, in Pound's shadow.

But the translator after Pound enters a field fraught with danger. Discussion of translation rarely fails to generate the kind of heat that can make Vladimir Nabokov wish to record his 'utter disgust with the general attitude, amoral and philistine, towards literalism'.[3] This is an age of translating-machines, of the scientific study of languages, an age which stresses, and achieves, greater reaches of literal accuracy than ever before. Yet, words, phrases, syntax and verse forms are impregnated with, as George Steiner puts it, 'complex traditions of behaviour'; therefore, 'translation is either an honest crib, a crutch to be laid beside the dictionary, or it is an imitation, a re-enactment of parallel gestures in a medium radically transformed. . . . An act of translation is an act of love. Where it fails, through immodesty or blurred perception, it traduces. Where it succeeds it transfigures.'[4] Admirable sentiments, in a way: Steiner's words recall Shelley's ascription to translators of a more than ordinary vanity.[5] But the problem is that acts of love are often indistinguishable from acts of gross immodesty.

Lowell's case offers additional difficulties. His 'imitations' claim a merit by their placing in their context over and above the merit they hold in isolation; and, as he admits more than once in the Introduction to *Imitations*, he has allowed himself more than an ordinary 'imitators' ' freedom. He has shortened and lengthened poems, by omitting or adding lines, and even whole stanzas; thus he has left out one-third of Rimbaud's 'The Drunken Boat', and has added two stanzas to Rilke's 'A Roman Sarcophagus', and even, in renderings of poems by Montale and Pasternak, amalgamated poems by the original authors. In a review of A. E. Watts' version of Ovid's *Metamorphoses*, Lowell quite clearly placed himself on the side of the 'risk-takers', those who aim for 'poetry' at the expense of academic accuracy; of

3. *Encounter*, February 1966, p. 80.
4. *Literature and Silence*, pp. 298–9.
5. In 'A Defence of Poetry'.

Watts' translation he said that it was 'admirable, steady, civilised —and impossible', for 'the resources of rhetoric cannot be explored by academic piety and a photostat exhibition of devices and tropes'.[6] One of those translators who offer a work that in some sense occupies a midway territory between them and the author they are translating, Lowell expects concessions from the original.

Lowell's *Imitations* is a book which he wishes to be regarded as a 'sequence, one voice running through many personalities, contrasts and repetitions'.[7] Certainly, there are countless vigorous phrases which are interchangeable from one poet to the next:

> I shiver. A dead whiteness spreads over
> my body, trickling pinpricks of sweat.
> I am greener than the greenest green grass—
> I die![8]

—as it happens, this is from an 'imitation' of Sappho. The book offers a particular view of European culture and poetry from Homer to Pasternak, with Baudelaire as the pivot of the whole proceedings; the poems are presented in chronological order, apart from Rilke's 'Pigeons', which acts as a coda. With only a few exceptions Lowell doesn't introduce us to unfamiliar poets or poems, which distinguishes his work from Pound's in this field; but the omissions are significant. There is no Vergil or Ovid; but *The Mills of the Kavanaughs* contains 'buried' versions of these two poets, though Lowell admits that Ovid is the one Classical writer almost unrenderable into English. There is no Horace and no Juvenal; but the omission is made up in the later *Near the Ocean*. One suspects that Lowell finds the Latin writers so near to his own temper and concerns that he felt they justified separate treatment in another book. There is no Dante; but here again, *Near the Ocean* partly makes up the leeway, and in one sense, the whole of Lowell's work is an acknowledgement of Dante's subtle force. On the whole, he has chosen poets who offer a particular honesty of self-revelation, so that the book is

6. *Kenyon Review*, XVII, Spring 1955, p. 317.
7. *I.*, p. xi.
8. *I.*, p. 3.

an extension into new fields of the 'confessional' impulse of *Life Studies*; the versions of Rilke, in particular, capture something of the earlier book's tone of detached portraiture:

> There's absence in the eyes. The brow's in touch
> with something far. Now distant boyishness
> and seduction shadow his enormous lips,
> the slender aristocratic uniform
> with its Franz Josef braid; both the hands bulge
> like gloves upon the sabre's basket hilt.
> The hands are quiet, they reach out toward nothing—[9]

Lowell avoids archaisms and archaic verse-forms. On occasions, the voice rises to rhetoric; but more often, it is an idiomatic voice, sometimes speaking with a greater directness than in Lowell's original poetry.

In *Imitations*, 'the dark and against the grain stand out',[10] as Lowell puts it. Its themes are: pain, violence, the abuse of power, the agonies of the artistic life. The first poem, 'The Killing of Lykaon', is an extract from Homer's *Iliad*; Lowell's Achilles is less the Greek hero than a luster after blood:

> You must die,
> and die and die and die, until the blood
> of Hellas and Patroklos is avenged,
> killed by the running ships when I was gone.[11]

In this book, the Trojan War is a recurring image of man's senseless urge for butchery. Lowell tries to capture an Homeric amplitude with his use of a version of the medieval alliterative line, and of epic inversions, and yet the effect is stilted, rather than elevated:

> God's will was working out,
> from that time when first fell apart fighting
> Atrides, king of men, and that god, Achilles . . .[12]

9. *I.*, p. 98.   10. *I.*, p. xi.
11. *I.*, p. 2.   12. *I.*, p. 1.

With poetry remote from him in time, Lowell's intention seems to have been to strip the poetry as much as possible of its in-built rhetoric or lyricism and hope that something moving would emerge; at least, this seems to have happened with his versions of Villon. One can see why Villon appealed to him: the harrowing view of age, lost laments for youth, a physical, unsentimental directness. His version of Villon's 'Ballad for the Dead Ladies' begins:

> Say in what land, or where
> is Flora, the lovely Roman,
> Andromeda, or Helen,
> far lovelier,
> or Echo, who would answer
> across the brook or river—
> her beauty was more than human!
> Oh where is last year's snow?[13]

This is flat and unlyrical, but to good effect. The same desire to achieve a stark directness is evident in Lowell's renderings of three Leopardi poems, which invite comparison with Pound's Leopardi versions; there are several fine phrases and stanzas:

> Then all's at peace;
> the lights are out;
> I hear the rasp of shavings,
> and the rapping hammer hammer
> of the carpenter, working all night
> by lanternlight—
> hurrying and straining himself
> to increase his savings
> before the whitening day.[14]

And yet, at the same time, we are aware that the effect of other passages in these Leopardi versions is very unlike that of the original. Leopardi's ponderings on infinity and his nihilism, which are contained, and to some extent stiffened and

13. *I.*, p. 15.
14. *I.*, p. 27.

67

unsentimentalised by the formal perfection of the Italian, with an assonance unobtainable in English, are dissipated by Lowell into free verse, and by fussy passages of added detail; and the emotions are too highly-coloured, with the nihilism and despair held in a kind of limbo.

For many readers, Lowell's success or failure as an 'imitator' will be decided by his renderings of Baudelaire.[15] Baudelaire is both a summation of past traditions, and at the birth of modern poetry, so that any view of European poetry over the centuries has to face up to him. But so much of the French poet refuses to be translated: his 'ennui', his world-weariness, often become a febrile or over-heated, post-Freudian thing in the hands of his translators, as in Lowell's version of 'To the Reader':

> Like the poor lush who cannot satisfy,
> we try to force our sex with counterfeits,
> die drooling on the deliquescent tits,
> mouthing the rotten orange we suck dry.[16]

Or the exploration of the destructive forces within man comes across without that decorum that contains it in the original. So often in Lowell's Baudelaire versions, we get a Madame Tussaud's of exaggerated horrors, and the nobility, pride, pity and tenderness with which Baudelaire so often balances the negative impulses in his poetry are nowhere. 'The Voyage'—that great poem about man's eternal restlessness, his urge for self-discovery —loses its universality in Lowell's hectic contemporaneity:

> old maids who weep, playboys who live each hour,
> state banquets loaded with hot sauces, blood and trash,
> ministers sterilized by dreams of power,
> workers who love their brutalizing lash.[17]

15. Lowell's Baudelaire 'imitations' also appear in a glossy art-book version, with illustrations by Sidney Nolan, *The Voyage and Other Versions of Poems by Baudelaire*.

There is a particularly scathing attack on Lowell's Baudelaire versions by May Daniels, 'A Matter of Translation', in *The Critical Survey*, Winter 1971, pp. 234–8.

16. *I.*, p. 46.

17. *I.*, p. 70.

And most importantly, Lowell has sacrificed Baudelaire's sense of firmly-maintained hope at the end of this poem. One feels that Baudelaire has made more concessions to his translator than any other original poet in *Imitations*, and those who cherish a traditional view of Baudelaire, or those who stress literal accuracy above all, will be shocked.

For many readers of *Imitations*, the successes will be the versions of Montale and Pasternak. In his Introduction, Lowell refers to his discovery that Montale was 'strong in simple prose and could be made still stronger in free verse'. This is precisely what his versions offer:

> A dense white cold of maddened moths
> swaggers past parapet and lamp,
> shaking a sheet upon the earth,
> crackling like sugar underfoot.[18]

The alternative to 'the dark and against the grain' is in Lowell's versions of Pasternak. The latter's particular distinction as a poet was to imbue traditional 'poetic' themes, such as the return of spring, with conversational and prosaic strengths. He strove to convey the world of appearances with an uncluttered spontaneity, and yet catch the interior life of an event or image. In a deeply-Russian, unallegorical, and unromantic way, nature is for him a place of affirmations and values, and a mirror to an urban world and its relationships, a gallery of manscapes. Lowell responds to Pasternak's challenge well:

> Like a lassoed buffalo, the forest
> is noosed in the ropes of shrill feathered throats—
> a wrestler, all gratuitous muscle,
> caught in the pipes of the grand organ.[19]

Perhaps there is a moral here, for Russian is the only language of the book that Lowell claims no knowledge of. It is in the Pasternak 'imitations' that the whole book's dedication to

18. *I.*, p. 113.
19. *I.*, p. 137.

Elizabeth Bishop becomes clear: she shares Pasternak's ability to see the clearly-perceived object as in a state of miraculous candour.

The best passages in *Imitations* are those where Lowell is content to let the originals speak for themselves. His distinction between 'meaning' and 'tone' is, as C. Chadwick[20] has pointed out, hardly a valid one, the two being so interpenetrated. He is anything but that 'gaunt, graceless literalist' plying his 'trade'[21] Nabokov comes down in favour of, but at least *Imitations* is rarely dull, the fault of most books of poetry translations. Perhaps it is time to bury the old controversy and accept the need for versions of several kinds.

At the time he was putting together his *Imitations*, Lowell was also facing 'the longer, less concentrated problems' of translating Racine's *Phèdre*.[22] The main impulse seems to have been the technical challenge: 'no [earlier] translator has had the gifts or the luck to bring Racine into our culture'.[23] The last phrase puts the emphasis right, for it is more than a question of finding an English equivalent for Racine's famous style, or solving the problem of his alexandrines: it involves finding a home for a writer in a culture which has only a limited tradition of High or Classical Tragedy. *Phèdre* is a particularly apt choice. It is a European classic familiar to many English speakers in the original French; it is itself an adaptation, being based on Euripides' *Hippolytus* (Claudel once described Euripides as the Greek Baudelaire), and there is thus the incentive of bringing together three historical periods in one play; and it has a pervasive sea imagery. But the principal attraction is in its plot: its themes of incest and adultery lend themselves to interpretations stressing psychological, biological, and hereditary factors—a peculiarly modern emphasis. Yet Lowell's description of Racine in his version of Baudelaire's 'The Swan' suggests that he might not be the best man for the task:

20. 'Meaning and Tone', in *Essays in Criticism*, XIII, 1963, pp. 432–5.
21. *Encounter*, February 1966, p. 80.
22. *I.*, p. xiii.
23. *PH.*, p. 8.

> those grander years,
> when Racine's tirades scourged our greasy Seine.[24]

This gives a satirical emphasis uncharacteristic of Racine.

Lowell has kept faithfully to the structure of Racine's play, and all the characters and speeches are there; where he has allowed himself considerable liberties is in the tone and meaning. It is this odd conjunction of faithfulness and licence that ultimately ruins his version. Firstly, the presentation of the heroine. At times, she comes across as something like Shakespeare's Cleopatra:

> Tear off these gross, official rings, undo
> these royal veils. They drag me to the ground.
> Why have you frilled me, laced me, crowned me, and
>   wound
> my hair in turrets?[25]

On other occasions she is a Lady Macbeth. A much more physical, lustful and obsessed character than Racine's, she is a post-Freudian Phèdre, whose passion is described thus:

> capricious burnings flickered through my bleak
> abandoned flesh.[26]

Her passion—but also its delicate balancing with remorse and shame—inheres in Racine's language. It would be difficult for a literalist translator to render; but Lowell pushes it in a quite Websterian direction.

Racine's verse of alexandrine couplets, with few run-on lines, is a mixture of ease and civility. Faced with the two extremes of slavishly writing end-stopped couplets, or free verse, Lowell's choice was the only one: run-on, rhyming couplets, with the rhymes not too obtrusive. In practice, however, his excessive use of run-on lines destroys whatever decorum there is in the original and so often, he betrays unease with couplets:

24. *I.*, p. 57.
25. *PH.*, p. 18.
26. *PH.*, p. 25.

> And yet your tears and words bewildered me,
> and so endangered my tranquillity,
> at last I spoke. Nurse, I shall not repent,
> if you will leave me the passive content
> of dry silence and solitude.[27]

Racine's French is at home with abstractions and simple descriptions; when Lowell says in his introduction that Racine has few memorable lines, he seems to be unappreciative of his original's straightforward effects. He can't help but pack his lines with detail in a way that is very like Lowell, but unlike Racine; if one overdoes the concreteness and the descriptive 'physicality', one loses the tension and inevitability which are the glories of Racinian tragedy. Individually, these passages are often very acceptable:

> he seemed to blanch
> and toss with terror like an aspen branch.[28]

But there are several mixed metaphors which are just puzzling.

Phèdre is a tragedy of guilt—guilt in seventeenth-century Catholic terms. But Lowell sees guilt in post-Freudian, post-Kinsey, and American Puritan terms: it is Freud crossed with Cotton Mather, Jonathan Edwards and Hawthorne, and with a dash of Emily Dickinson. Chastity becomes 'primness'; a noble bearing, a 'reserved and cool' attitude; a strange madness, 'uncertainty'; dignity, 'poise'; will, 'self-control'; crime, 'defection'; hatred, 'displeasure'; wounding pride and rudeness, 'shyness'. Psychological motivation is substituted for myth; sexual unbalance and frustration, Lowell announces, is the reason for all these maimed, racked, disordered bodies, and Racine's unique energy expresses itself here in a frenetic giddyness. How often the words 'nerve' and 'nervous' appear in Lowell's version; thus, the original's 'mortal ennui' becomes 'nervous langour'. But what is totally wrong is the special kind of self-consciousness displayed by all the major characters:

> Phaedra: My emotions shake my breast.[29]

27. *PH.*, p. 26. 28. *PH.*, p. 61. 29. *PH.*, p. 18.

This example is particularly bad: it is Phèdre's first entrance and Racine makes it clear that she is suffering from a physical complaint the nature of which she doesn't understand. Any suggestion that she does, would destroy the impression of her being Venus' victim. In Racine, characters are racked by the thought of confessing themselves to others, and even to themselves; but Lowell's characters do it willingly, and any sense of the arbitrariness with which the gods operate and with which passions arise from within is thus lost.

Perhaps what is most deeply wrong in all this is: it insults the audience. Lowell's additions and interpretations imply we might be bored by Racine's 'simplicities', or that the Phèdre we have grown up with in the theatre is somehow stuffy and unworthy of our attentions. So Lowell is prepared to sacrifice Racinian qualities for character-drawing in a naturalistic sense. Here is Aricie speaking at the beginning of Act Two:

> Goose, you've lost your feeble wits!

> My dear, your news
> is only frivolous gossip, I refuse
> to hope.[30]

Is this what Lowell means by 'unRacinian humour'?[31] Aricie has become a spoilt Hollywood matron.

Very unsure of himself in Racine's world of absolute values, Lowell unavailingly tries to substitute modern equivalents for innocence, pride, chastity, virtue, honour, duty and service. He is also unhappy about the play as myth; in his version, the classical framework becomes mere paraphernalia; the gods, ornaments; and Phèdre's, Theseus', and Hippolytus' special relationships to their pasts is not made believable. In Racine, Neptune is a real monster; in Lowell, the monsters are within. But as well as losing their relationship to the gods, Lowell's characters lose their social roles: they are solely private people. Thus, Theseus is reduced in size to a 'lascivious eulogist of any belle'—though he sometimes sounds like Leontes in *The Winter's Tale*. We lose all the Racinian tension between a man's power

30. *PH.*, pp. 29, 30.   31. *PH.*, p. 8.

in the world and his helplessness in the face of private torments and the whims of the gods.

What of the play's ending? Many readers will be horrified by Lowell's version of Phèdre's last speech: we are denied the sense of a simple, restored harmony and the return of light. Light is a central image in Racine's play, representing both Hippolytus' innocence, and the moral order; without this representation in Lowell, it is largely decorative. Elegance, logic, dignity: all are missing from Lowell's version.

In 'Maule's Curse', Yvor Winters says that the New England inheritance was 'an inheritance of confusion':[32] Lowell's trilogy of plays, *The Old Glory*, takes a long, hard look at this confusion. Coming from the same year as *For the Union Dead*, it echoes the poems: tyrants and tyrannicides are interchangeable; the crowd denotes fear; rebellions are death-seeking. A reviewer in the *Christian Science Monitor* aptly called the trilogy an 'heroic act of dissenting patriotism'[33] and one can perhaps see in it the erosion of hope in the Kennedy years. The plays are tragedies of idealism; Lowell has said America is 'the Ahab story of having to murder evil: and you may murder all the good with it if it gets desperate enough to struggle'.[34]

The appearance of two of the plays on an off-Broadway stage in 1964[35] was greeted with some enthusiasm by critics, as offering the possibility of a new kind of American poetic drama, one more contemporary in flavour than the poetic dramas of such poet-playwrights as Archibald MacLeish and William Carlos Williams. Robert Brustein welcomed them as satisfying a desire for 'a more ample kind of acting', and heralding 'the eventual supersession of something worn-out and sterile by a force of genuine vitality and intelligence'.[36] In the event, Brustein's hopes were not ful-

32. *In Defense of Reason*, London (Routledge) 1960, p. 174.

33. Albert J. Gelpi, 'He Holds America to Its Ideals', in *Christian Science Monitor*, 16 December 1965, p. 11.

34. *Alvarez*, p. 42.
An American soldier is reported as saying of the destruction of a Vietnamese village: 'We had to destroy it in order to save it.'

35. For details, see Jonathan Miller's 'Director's Note' to the plays. *O.G.*, pp. viii–xiv.

36. *Seasons of Discontent: dramatic opinions 1959–65*, London (Cape) 1966, p. 20 and p. 252.

filled. Given the present state of the American theatre, it is hardly surprising. *The Old Glory* is static, austere, formal, pageant-like drama, unlikely to arouse a mass audience—which, in any case, is traditionally unhappy both with one-acters and contemporary poetic drama; and the trilogy's experimental touches are hardly geared to interest avant-garde theatre-goers, being mainly derived from American and German expressionist drama of the 1920's. As history plays, they stand somewhere between the 'poetry' of *Murder in the Cathedral* and the 'pageantry' of Maxwell Anderson, but in their serious conception and uncompromisingly difficult themes, they suggest parallels with the work of John Arden in England.

All three plays are about communities in which the democratic veneer is cracked by rebellion and violence, and the cruel wielding of repressive authority. The pattern is similar: a slow, steady build-up, during which there is an aura of calm and lassitude, and then the sudden eruption of the forces of a primitive darkness; an outsider—Endecott, Robin, Delano—is drawn painfully into a course of action he doesn't understand, and would formerly have deplored, and into an exhibition of misguided energies as a means of escaping the nagging doubts and ambiguities in which he has been enmeshed. The trilogy poses a question of strong contemporary relevance: how does it happen that democracy is so repressive?

'Endecott and the Red Cross' tells the story of a seventeenth-century Puritan governor of Salem whose religion moves him to oppose manifestations of spiritual laxity, for which he blames the representatives of the Cavaliers and the Church of England in America; in particular, he takes a stand against maypole-dancing. Lowell makes the governor a much milder figure than the one whom Hawthorne calls 'the severest Puritan who laid the rock foundation of New England', and a much more ambiguously-motivated one. By his own confession, he is a 'suit of empty armour', a former military man whom administration has softened, and he is caught in the cross-fire of several ways of life. After a period of hesitation, and racked by a disorder within him, he chooses the road of oppression of the disorder he sees around him.

Of the three plays, it is the nearest to straightforward naturalism; but it is the songs and dances of the revellers which liven

75

up what would otherwise be a very thin, dull play. This is its weakness: it convinces neither as a naturalistic play, nor does it offer the stylised, ritualised interest of the other plays. But it is open to question whether Hawthorne can ever be satisfactorily transferred to the stage. His lack of hard edges, his dependence on a sense of mystery, remoteness and wonder, lend themselves to the risk of over-simplification, for drama—any kind—depends on a certain precision of outline.

'My Kinsman, Major Molineux' takes many of the themes of the first play into the next century. Respectability has hit Boston: Indians and maypole-dancers are a thing of legend now, and the forest frontier has been replaced by the Atlantic. The decline of Puritanism signalled by Endecott's waverings has become fact, and commerce is in the ascendant. To the single (English) flag of the first play is now added the rattlesnake flag of the colonists. The action takes place on what Hawthorne calls an 'evening of ambiguity and weariness'. Robin, a country youth, and his younger brother, are in Boston seeking out their cousin, the Major, who commands the Redcoats in Boston, and are precipitated into the throes of the American Revolution. Robin fails to make sense of a very dangerous political situation where violence—as in Arden's *Serjeant Musgrave's Dance*—can erupt at any minute and engulf all. The American nation is being born out of hatred and hypocrisy. Robin confuses the birth with freedom, and is drawn into the mob's violence. At the end Molineux dies, and a red light spreads over the stage; it is as if only blood can satiate the thirst of the new American child. The conclusion is that, where innocent and guilty are treated alike, the real power lies with the undiscriminating mob.

Lowell has moved away from the original Hawthorne story in several directions. In providing Robin with a confidant, he has translated Robin's dangerous innocence into a simple kind of naivety:

> I liked the way
> the soldiers smiled. I wonder how
> anyone could distrust a soldier[37]

37. *O.G.*, p. 70.

—something much nearer to the 'innocents abroad' of American mythology. Hawthorne tells us that Robin's mind 'Kept vibrating between fancy and reality'; Lowell has pushed the story unilaterally in the direction of fancy and absurdity. Jonathan Miller's production, with its use of masks, colours, lighting and cartoon elements in the manner of Hogarth and Gilray, has helped Lowell here. Furthermore, the city's mythical role is much more pronounced in the play: Boston is the City of the Dead. The political implications—strongly marked in Lowell—are only outlined in Hawthorne.

It is the most stylised play of the trilogy. This is an Alice in Wonderland world in which the characters are part-mythical, as with the ferryman/Charon, and part-caricature, as with the Clergyman; all of them, apart from Robin and his brother, are dressed in black and white, have pasted faces, and powdered wigs. But some of the effects are the most tedious ones of expressionism; for example, the double-facedness of Boston is expressed in the Clergyman holding up the English and Revolutionary flags, waiting for the wind to tell him which way to fly; there is a man with a face of two colours—a simplified version of the nightmare character in Hawthorne.

With the third play of the trilogy, 'Benito Cereno', the American Republic is well-established. Lowell updates the story to 'about 1800',[38] and re-names the American boat, *President Adams*: in 1800, Jefferson defeated John Adams in the presidential election, and sealed the triumph of cosmopolitanism and French Enlightenment ideas in the context of the consolidation of American nationhood. This time, the flags are those of the American Republic and Spain. The first action of the play is the saluting of the American flag, which now represents not rebellion, but authority: this is the period of American imperialism, and 'America is wherever her flag lives'. The Spanish flag is irreverently treated as a shaving napkin.

Melville's 'Benito Cereno' is one of the most powerful short novels in existence. It achieves its effects by methods very different from Hawthorne's. Melville's prose is harder, more precise, less given to romantic langours than Hawthorne's, with many

38. In a letter to the *Village Voice* (19 November 1964), Lowell said: 'The play is set about 1803, in Jefferson's time.' The text says 'about 1800'.

superbly-managed ironies. The story is simple in outline: Captain Amassa Delano, one Independence Day, meets a Spanish vessel whose captain, Benito Cereno, is held captive by his cargo of slaves, who have revolted. Refusing to believe what he sees, Delano (another innocent) exposes himself to danger, until the truth becomes inescapable; the moment of truth is when Don Aranda's skeleton is thrust at him, in a scene recalling the climax of *Serjeant Musgrave's Dance*. Then Delano's veneer of benevolence drops and he responds with violence. Social order in the play is invested in Delano; the forces of rebellion in Babu, the leader of the negro slaves.

All the confusions, hypocrisies and ambiguities of American behaviour meet in the figure of the pompous American captain. He believes himself to represent a quintessential Americanness —and indeed does exemplify a peculiarly American cheerful, but shallow pragmatism—and yet he carries a Spanish name, as Molineux carried a French one; a Northerner, who shares Lowell's father's 'unspoiled faith in the superior efficiency of northern nations',[39] he admires Southern aristocratic manners, and behaves towards negroes like a white racialist; a disciplinarian, he yet advocates 'a little regulated corruption'; a convinced believer in the superior abilities of American seamanship and customs, he professes a worldly feeling for foreign customs. Symbolic of his isolation from reality is the embalming gear he carries on board ship. The play consists of an extraordinary series of episodes in which Babu indulges in his power by taunting Delano with the truth he refuses to accept.

Considerable travesty has been done to the Delano of Melville's tale[40] who—innocent though he was—had dignity; 'a man of such native simplicity as to be incapable of satire or irony' is Melville's description. Lowell's Delano recalls Harkness in '91 Revere Street'. It is difficult to believe that his mind is capable of concocting the several passages of Melville prose-into-poetry

39. *L.S.*, p. 25.

Philip Cooper, in *The Autobiographical Myth of Robert Lowell*, p. 75, sees something of Colonel Shaw of Lowell's poem 'For the Union Dead' in Captain Delano.

40. Robert Ilson, ' "Benito Cereno" from Melville to Lowell', in *Salmagundi*, I, iv, 1966–67, pp. 78–86, and reprinted in *Parkinson*, pp. 135–42, offers a detailed comparison of story and play.

which come out as a kind of nervous tic whenever he looks through his telescope; presumably we are to believe these passages well up from his subconscious? Yet his 'poetry' is more appropriately of the clichéd order which can describe the American flag as the most beautiful woman in South America. It is as if there are two Delanos: the weak, stupid, naively-optimistic, credulous, unworldly one; and the one who shows perception, and acts and speaks, as he is aware, as an image of America:

> Real life is a simple monotonous thing.
>
> When a country loses heart, it's easier to live.
>
> We are like two dreams meeting head-on.[41]

More of these *aperçus* might have saved him as a human being. Delano's progress is made to stand for an hundred years of lost democratic ideals from Melville's time to ours.

In confronting Babu, Melville's Delano was confronting the evil in himself and in the world; this Babu is a silent figure who declines to explain his motives. In Lowell's presentation of Babu, we come much nearer to the realities of white–negro relationships, particularly at the end of the play when Babu gives an account of the reasons for his actions, and Delano's moral duplicity is revealed. Clearly, when Babu says, 'Yankee Master understand me. The future is with us', he speaks with the accents of the Black Panthers confronting whitey, and his replacement of Artufel has clear parallels with the demotion of Martin Luther King in black extremist circles. But Lowell has moved the tale into an even wider context. The Babu who dies in a hail of bullets from Delano's gun is all those small underdeveloped nations confronting western military might. Delano's and the play's final line—'This is your future', as the bullets fly—is an equal truth to Babu's; Delano has turned the negro he once admired into a gook.

The Old Glory is historical and political drama. The one purpose that unites the three plays is that of showing how America, plagued by a sense of destiny, has always been in a posture of rejection of those things which have later re-appeared.

41. *O.G.*, pp. 150, 155, 162, respectively.

In all three plays, Lowell has taken the skeleton of his stories and characters from the originals—but little else. Whereas both Hawthorne and Melville see ambiguity as endemic in the human psyche, Lowell sees it as a duplicity hidden by surface clichés, something to be exposed and burned away.

'I think my own concerns and worries and those of the time seep in':[42] thus Lowell claims personal and contemporary relevance for his prose version of Aeschylus' play, *Prometheus Bound*. Clearly, he has been throughout his life a Prometheus himself, chained to the rock of his family's, Boston's and New England's pasts: the myth is thus buried deep in much that he has written.

At the political level, the Prometheus myth is about political evolution and Caesarism: Zeus and Prometheus are the New Order of the gods—the phrase has a stark twentieth century ring about it. A one-time liberal authoritarian, Zeus, now become totalitarian and claiming historical determinism for his actions, imprisons a former ally, Prometheus, who persists in championing the old liberal virtues; it is Caesar versus Brutus; Robespierre versus Danton; Lenin/Stalin versus Trotsky. At first sight, it is the political interpretation of the myth that Lowell has gone for, and the political parallels with the state of contemporary America are constantly apparent: 'the river of violence now runs across this land like a scar'. In the fate of Lowell's Prometheus, we recognise the tragedy of democracy and of the doomed progressive in the post-John F. Kennedy years. Yet the play was given a seventeenth-century setting by its first producer, Jonathan Miller. This has obvious advantages; the play needed a particular historical setting, rather than a timeless one of gods and goddesses, to give it body. The seventeenth-century background, with its sombre setting and costumes, gives the play a low-keyed, restrained quality, where some of the speeches and ideas tend to take off into heady, rhetorical flights. But the choice of this particular century is more than theatrically apt. For Yeats, 'The mischief began at the end of the seventeenth

42. Blurb to *P.B.*

In *Encounter*, May 1973, p. 67, Lowell describes democracy in Promethean terms: 'The Americans' democratic faith is suddenly at bottom. One ought to be glad to lose this angel, devil, firebringer, Milton's rebel, the first American.'

century when man became passive before a mechanised nature';[43] for Erich Heller, it is 'the century of cosmic tidiness'.[44] Lowell's play is about the world that post-Renaissance man has made.

A play whose main character remains chained to a rock—in theory, if not in stage practice—for the whole length presents an obvious challenge to an audience's ability to remain interested. Moreover, Lowell has sacrificed considerable dramatic interest by piling up most of the sympathy in Prometheus' favour; in Aeschylus, the scales of sympathy are more nearly balanced between Zeus and Prometheus, and the latter has to learn through suffering and is rebuked for his pride. Lowell has chosen to pitch the play as a mixture of dramatic monologue, lyric drama, and play of ideas. A sinner in the hands of an angry god, Prometheus illustrates the Second Voice's dictum that 'intelligence is suffering': he is chained to himself, his own burden of consciousness. Goethe defined the poet's distinctive gift from the gods as the power to say what he suffered; Prometheus is a politician who has been forced to become a poet. Like the protagonist of the title-poem of *For the Union Dead*, he longs for an earlier inarticulate state of organic existence: 'I think I should have been more loyal to the idiocy of things'.

Yet it is a very unmoving play. Occasionally, Lowell offers us bits of 'real' characterisation, as in his picture of the time-serving Ocean, who is very Shavian: 'A telling word, a timely touch, that's my strategy.' But so many characters are locked in the 'mud' of inaction. Io is probably the only character to fulfil a truly dramatic function; her long speeches ring authentic with rich, animal life:

> I remember that walk—hot brown grass like an oven
> under my feet, excited cattle, nudging against me, and
> rolling up their eyes. At every step, I felt the slow
> swish and slap of a tasseled tail. The air was thick and
> rich as hay. The whole pasture lay like a huge
> panting body.[45]

This section of the play is its one real success.

43. Quoted in *Language and Silence*, p. 228.
44. *The Disinherited Mind*, Cambridge (Bowes & Bowes) 1952, pp. 268–9.
45. *P.B.*, p. 36.

Lowell has avoided both archaisms and the chic modernity of many twentieth-century dramatisations of Greek myths. There are some excellent individual lines ('I hear something, a whirring of birds. The air is sinewed with their fragile wings') and an effective use of atmosphere: it is a play of light and heat, sky, sea and wind, loneliness and silence. But what is left of Aeschylus? Lowell doesn't offer the kind of re-shaping of old forms that *Murder in the Cathedral* offers; his Chorus of sea-birds has neither lyrical nor dramatic excitement. Aeschylus' play is really an evolutionary play, and the long accounts of Io's and Prometheus' sufferings get their point from the audience's realisation that Zeus is eventually going to have to compromise. But in Lowell's play evolution has terminated. However, it is an interesting play because it is the most directly personal of his three attempts to date at drama, and because it is a philosophical—if not very dramatic—statement of ideas in his 'sixties poetry.[46]

46. An interesting sidelight on Lowell's play, and on his 'Waking Early Sunday Morning' in *N.O.*, is thrown by Charles Tomlinson's poem 'Prometheus', in *The Way of a World*, London (O.U.P.) 1969, pp. 4–5, which rejects the kind of extremism Lowell has been associated with. Instead of Lowell's apocalyptic 'volcanic cone' and 'monotonous sublimities' ('Waking Early Sunday Morning'), Tomlinson's poem offers a 'cooled world of incessant codas' and 'the cruel mercy of solidities'.

5   The Unforgivable Landscape

The end of *Life Studies* found Lowell faced with conformity as the apparent price of survival—the lives of the 'young Republican' and the 'book-worming' poet of 'Memories of West Street and Lepke'. But if the last lines of 'Home After Three Months Away'—

> I keep no rank nor station.
> Cured, I am frizzled, stale and small[1]

—imply a grudging acceptance of reduced perspectives, 'Flabby, bald, lobotomized' (of Czar Lepke) touches the spiritual death it can lead to. 'Skunk Hour' was perhaps the safety-valve: its 'ambiguous affirmation' offered an alternative to the conventional life, and its technical achievement was a welcome augury for Lowell's future development.

With the next book—*For the Union Dead* (1964)—Lowell trod a difficult tightrope beyond the already considerable achievement of *Life Studies*: this had been in the writing about personal and family matters with a new immediacy, and in the forging of a new style—one which Lowell has described in terms of conversation, prose, photography and 'loose formality'.[2] But the movement away from the early poetry's strict forms and doctrines, whether an idiosyncratic Catholicism or a compulsive Calvinism, had left a lack of urgency and purpose about many of the *Life Studies* poems, as if Lowell had moved into new areas of poetic experience without fully working out the thematic and formal implications: so many of the poems offer mere immersion in the flux of experience, with the only shaping factors in the thread of certain imagery, and in the highly-wrought structure of the book

1. *L.S.*, p. 98.
2. Alvarez interview in *The Review*, 8, August 1963, p. 37. Lowell says here that he was 'imitating the loose formality' of Elizabeth Bishop's style.

as a whole. However, *Imitations* must have been an important stage on the way to the next book, with Lowell trying himself out within the limits of another writer's themes and forms; it opened the way to an exploration of a wider world than that of family history and, as with Yeats at a similar stage in his career, a new mythology: a more personal one than that of the 'forties, and more related to experience in the present. In practical terms, the result is that *For the Union Dead* has a whole new range of subjects and themes, larger social statements, deeper psychological probings, and a closer examination of the artist's role. At the same time, the new expansion is largely an effort to define the precisely human for the protagonist of the new poems has painfully to recognise that the natural and metaphysical worlds are no longer his to exploit and dominate.

In *For the Union Dead*, the context is now one of personal pain and turmoil, and of a recognition of the impermanence of all values in a nuclear age. This partly explains Lowell's vulnerability in the new book ('At fifty we're so fragile, / a feather . . .'), and why the apparent unassumingness of such a figure as Alfred Corning Clark takes on a larger significance. A minor elegy about a rich friend whose life seemed on the surface a failure and waste, the Clark poem has a familiar ring:

> You read the *New York Times*
> every day at recess,
> but in its dry
> obituary, a list
> of your wives, nothing is news,
> except the ninety-five
> thousand dollar engagement ring
> you gave the sixth.[3]

But though Clark seems to step from the pages of *Life Studies*, he emerges as a hero of a new type. The gently-affectionate tone suggests some deep affinity between this low-keyed figure and the poet; in '91 Revere Street', Lowell says of himself: 'At school, however, I was extreme only in my conventional mediocrity, my colourless, distracted manner.' Lowell endures a difficult process

3. *F.U.D.*, p. 20.

of self-identification, barely disguised by the impassive language of 'I feel the pain. . . . I owe you something. . . . I was befogged . . you usually won.'[4] On the page, the poem lies still and disengaged, and like its subject

> motionless
> as a lizard in the sun.[5]

One of several poems in *For the Union Dead* in which the poet discovers himself in figures from the past, 'Alfred Corning Clark', shows Lowell searching for something more constructive than the apparently casual reminiscences of many of the *Life Studies* poems, or the violence of the 'raging memory [drooling] / Over the glory of past pools'[6] of an early poem. Both fascinated and imprisoned by memories, he seeks freedom through deliberate appropriations of them, and throughout the book, weaves patterns of recollection: 'Remember we sat on a slab of rock?'; 'Remember our lists of birds?'; 'Remember Summer?'; but the past has to be made the past again, 'thinning echoes' from another world. 'Beginning in wisdom, and ending in doubt' (a stoic turning of Frost's dictum) points to the present's stringent circumstances, and 'Everything's aground . . . Nothing catches fire' could almost act as a prescription for the new poetic.

Several poems are about the problem of facing a past which is both fuel for, and a deceptive gloss on, the present. 'The Scream' is full of elements of bright-eyed childhood perception:

> the horseshoes sailed through the dark,
> like bloody little moons,
> red-hot, hissing, protesting, . . .[7]

The child's world is a manic one of simple alternatives and connectives, but the primary colours constantly devolve into something sinister. The last verse could stand as a coda to *Life Studies*:

> . . . But they are all gone,
> those aunts and aunts, a grandfather,

4. *F.U.D.*, pp. 20–1.   5. *F.U.D.*, p. 21.
6. *P.*, p. 41.   7. *F.U.D.*, p. 8.

> a grandmother, my mother—
> even her scream—too frail
> for us to hear their voices long.[8]

'The Lesson' stresses the ambiguous dealings of Time: has all changed, or nothing? The poem's teasing repetitions suggest its author's early energies were homage to a false image of human uniqueness. In 'Those Before Us', the shapes of the past are seen in a kind of punning, myopic vision.

Part of Lowell's effort in *For the Union Dead* is towards establishing distinctions between the human and the non-human worlds. Man's purposes so often blur the dividing-lines, and his laws so often perpetrate injustices against the natural world. The idea of law and lawlessness is central in *For the Union Dead*. In early Lowell, Law was established society, evil in its exclusiveness, an appropriative world with an Old Testament instinct for possessions, and issuing in the divided conscience of the New England temper:

> Under one law,
> or two,
> to lie unsleeping,
> still sleeping on the battlefield . . .[9]

('Law')

In 'Law' in this latest book, Lowell builds on something touched on in the Naipaul interview: his desire as a child to escape the constraints of a Boston Sunday by fishing. (Lowell often uses images of fish and fishing to suggest a liberation from the restrictions of human society into nature.) Using details from Emerson's famous 'Concord Hymn', the poem is a commentary on New England's past efforts to bring natural, ethical, and spiritual values into some sort of unity, its constant failures, and the violence that so often underpinned these efforts: 'A Norman canal *shot* through *razored* green lawns'. But Nature remains inexorable, and in the last verse, words are piled like stones in a series of bleak adjectives and nouns:

8. *F.U.D.*, p. 9.
9. *F.U.D.*, p. 24.

       black, gray, green and blue,
     water, stone, grass and sky,[10]

—the elemental has its own imperatives.

Lowell has mellowed considerably since the days when he too adopted a Mosaic stance, and wrestled like an Ahab with natural forces. Now there is a forgiving mood ('Poor ghost, old love. . . . Poor rich boy . . . Poor country Berkeley. . . . Poor turtle, tortoise. . . .') which extends to ex-schoolfriends, figures of the past such as Jonathan Edwards, and wives. But another set of echoing phrases ties the warmer feelings to a hard acceptance of reality: 'No ease for the boy at the keyhole . . . No help from the fifth of Bourbon . . . No help for his body . . .' Indeed, in the book's first two poems, 'Water' and 'The Old Flame', poems about the break-up of a relationship, the compassionate is made to depend on an appraisal of what is elemental, secular and existential, to the extent of recognising that the natural world can't purify, fuse or heal, for the human condition is one of limitation and impermanence.

Although Lowell still retains the New England scene as a landscape of pain, banishment and loss, of 'suffering without purgation', the Maine of these poems no longer carries the simple emblematic role it had in *The Mills of the Kavanaughs*: a personal story of dislocation and alienation is played out against a landscape which remains recalcitrant to it. In 'Water', the rock is irreducible to symbol ('it was only the usual gray rock'), a fixed reality in spite of the sea's slow eroding processes, and the man-made erosions of the granite quarries.[11] But man's relationship to nature is always precarious: his houses cling 'like oyster-shells' and his weir consists of 'matchsticks'. The poem's half-rhymes ('bleak . . . stuck . . . stick . . . rock') seem fragile too, escape from one's grasp. Everything related to human perceptions and purposes is seen in an unromantic light: the rainbow colours

10. *F.U.D.*, p. 25.

11. In '91 Revere Street', Lowell uses an image of a rock in connection with memory: 'Major Mordecai Myers' portrait has been mislaid past finding, but out of my memories I often come on it in the setting of our Revere Street house, a setting now fixed in the mind, where it survives all the distortions of fantasy, all the blank befogging of forgetfulness. There, the vast number of remembered *things* remains rocklike.' *L.S.*, p. 21.

and purples decline into greys and greens, the 'hill of rock' from 'slab' to 'flake', in a process analogous to the crumbling of Jonathan Edwards' 'rock of hope' in another poem. In lines recalling the wish-fulfilment world at the end of Eliot's 'Prufrock', the apocalyptic struggle of an Ahab, and of Lowell's earlier poetry, is reduced to a dream-world where the woman of the poem imagines herself a mermaid, or tears hysterically at the barnacles in a futile effort to resist the steady progress of Time, 'flake after flake' (compare the 'minute by minute' of Yeats' 'Easter 1916'). The waters of baptism and purification are unavailing—

> In the end,
> the water was too cold for us[12]

—and the poem offers none of that sublime merging of personality with landscape that Whitmanite poetry invites. The whole curve of this bleakly-elemental poem's theme is in its first and last words: 'It . . . us': by recognising the otherness of the natural world, we can solder a human relationship—a theme of several poems in the book.

Erosion is an apt metaphor for Lowell's technical progress since the early 'fifties. The laconic utterance of 'Water' suggests a version of the New England poetic of Frost and Emily Dickinson; ordinary, colourless words are weighed, have a physical impact, the details cut into the mind sharply, and the short, taut line-units, in four-line stanzas (four- and five-line stanzas are a frequent pattern in the book) keep a firm control over the poem's emotional drive.

In spite of Lowell's own statement about his intentions ('an altered style, more impersonal matter, a new main artery of emphasis and inspiration'),[13] it is a mistake to think of him simply as 'depersonalising' his poetry after *Life Studies*. Rather, there is a range of new personae in *For the Union Dead*, which is perhaps an indirect outcome of Lowell's ironic and disengaged stance in *Imitations*, with its Symbolist stress on the poet as both craftsman

12. *F.U.D.*, p. 4.
13. In a letter quoted in M. L. Rosenthal, *The New Poets*, p. 67.

and suffering artist. The present book is about the artistic imagination in a much more direct way than *Life Studies*; the latter's four poems about writers come home to New England, and to Lowell himself. In 'Hawthorne' and 'Jonathan Edwards in Western Massachusetts', Lowell considers how much the New England writer owes to his tradition. The first is a taut, controlled portrait of a 'shy, distrustful ego'; one of the book's presiding muses, Hawthorne, with his diffidence and worldly failure relates to Clark:

> Leave him alone for a moment or two,
> and you'll see him with his head
> bent down, brooding, brooding,
> eyes fixed on some chip,
> some stone, some common plant,
> the commonest thing,
> as if it were the clue.[14]

The implicit hero of *For the Union Dead* is a survivor, victim, and sufferer at the edge of extreme self-consciousness and self-denigration, a figure trapped in a state of pained and heroic isolation.

In 'Jonathan Edwards in Western Massachusetts', Lowell makes Edwards talk of himself in a way that also suggests Clark: 'I am contemptible, stiff and dull'. The Edwards poem is Lowell's third on the subject, and the one invested with the most humanity. Though it uses several extracts from Edwards' writings, particularly his 'Personal Narrative' with its reflections on Bacon's Essay 'On Gardens', Lowell is now far enough away from the religious concerns that animated Edwards to see him with something approaching compassion. Principally, the poem is about the consequences of a loss of faith:

> Hope lives in doubt.
> Faith is trying to do without
>
> faith.[15]

14. *F.U.D.*, p. 39.
15. *F.U.D.*, p. 40.

—the stanza break and the lower casing neatly enact the loss o
faith, which Edwards saw around him, and which the moderr
world lives perpetually with. Edwards' faith declined because i
was too full of contradictions and anomalies, and after his death
lacked the force of a strong personality to sustain it. The poem':
conclusion is something like that of another poem, 'Fall 1961'
now in the twentieth century that 'we know how the world wil
end', we can have a truer sense of cosmic fate than Edwards
whose faith was built on a contemplation of individual mortality
learned from the spiders: 'you knew they would die'.

Lowell cannot now, like the 'poor country Berkeley', simply
see the world as the 'soul of God'. But treating Edwards and hi
faith in a forgiving manner, he allows that at the end of his life
—'old, exiled, and afraid'—in his Indian mission, Edwards wor
through to something like humanity. In the decline of his oal
of faith into a 'common piece of kindling', the arc of his affectior
widened to include both the dregs of society, and the nature he
had formerly appropriated for his metaphysical purposes (the
'loose winds' which used to 'greatly fix' his mind). The true
consummation of his faith was in his love for his Indian childrer
and for his wife, Sarah, and in his exchange of the Great Awakening for a sharing of Sarah's delight in the Great Being.

Lowell now sees the best, as well as the worst, in New England':
past religious traditions: no longer does he flail out ungenerously
at them. This more ambivalent attitude is at the heart of the title
poem: a major poem in both intention and achievement. The
poem's title, and the Latin motto, suggest another commemorative
effort on a Civil War theme in the tradition of Tate's 'Ode to the
Confederate Dead',[16] or James Russell Lowell's Harvard Ode
Yet, as usual with Lowell, his way of treating a conventiona
form, is an idiosyncratic one. A poem much admired for it:
social role as a commentary on the destruction of a city, and
on man's inhumanity to man in war and racial discrimination
perhaps it has not been seen enough as the climax to date o
Lowell's long-standing admiration for an ambiguous military
heroism.

16. For a comparison of Lowell's and Tate's Civil War poems, see E. T
Helmick, 'The Civil War Odes of Lowell and Tate', in *Georgia Review*, XXV
1971, pp. 51–5.

Two human constructs are juxtaposed throughout the poem—ditch and monument; the poem recounts the destruction of an older Boston—represented in the poem by the Civil War bronze relief of Colonel Shaw and the black 54th Massachusetts Regiment which he led—by steamshovels excavating underground car parks. The South Boston Aquarium—a double image for the personality and the past—has been entered by the bestial forces from without, which have released corresponding forces within the ego. The worlds of man and nature are subverted: the steamshovels are 'dinosaurs', the monument 'sticks like a fishbone in the city's throat', and the cars are 'finned'. A wrong relationship with nature issues in the sterility and infertility of a Waste Land:

> The bronze weathervane cod has lost half its scales.
> The airy tanks are dry.[17]

> Parking spaces luxuriate like civic
> sandpiles in the heart of Boston.[18]

In the midst of all this destruction stands the Colonel Shaw monument. A focus like the rock in 'Water', it is both an embodiment of the positives of the poem, and an ambivalent image. Though it testifies to man's destructiveness in war, it commemorates heroism, if a heroism of an unorthodox kind: Shaw and his regiment stood, not for the conventional military virtue of victory which is celebrated in the 'abstract', lifeless and conventional statues on village greens, but for civic virtues. Morally, Shaw relates forwards to the Civil Rights issue in the latter part of the poem; historically, he shares something of those uncompromising republican and puritan qualities imaged in the description of the churches:

> On a thousand small town New England greens,
> the old white churches hold their air
> of sparse, sincere rebellion.[19]

The aspirations of New England's past led to moral and civic achievements, and yet were invested in a rebellion against both

17. *F.U.D.*, p. 70.   18. *F.U.D.*, p. 70.   19. *F.U.D.*, p. 71.

God and nature. At the heart of the Colonel's philosophy there was something forbiddingly statuesque; his was a 'lonely courage',[20] as William James said, an aloof pride, an aristocratic refusal to bend his back, even when involved in the cause of negro freedom. The heart of the poem is in its definition of Shaw's tragic heroism:

> He rejoices in man's lovely,
> peculiar power to choose life and die.[21]

Now that the weathervane is broken, Shaw can act as a 'compass-needle' and guide; yet the compass points to destruction, for the man who 'winced' at pleasure now 'rejoices' in a code of conduct which issues in death. The puritan virtues that are commemorated in Shaw also produced the commercial greed that has devastated Boston, and the destruction of war. Yet Shaw does stand for a better relationship of true service—an older one linked with Old Boston—than that implied in the 'servility' of the cars in modern Boston, or the 'cowed compliance' of the aquarium fish.

The poem is built around opposing elements of constriction and release. The 'sparse, sincere rebellion' the poem details is in the context of a Statehouse surrounded by imprisoning girders, steamshovels working in a cage, a Colonel Shaw who is waiting for 'the blessed break' and who is 'out of bounds'; and the formal pattern beautifully enacts the complexity, with the poem's colloquial urge held in check by the tight stanzas. These stanzas are composed like bricks of different sizes and weights. With a metric combining free verse, iambic rhythm and prose these lines hold back with none of Lowell's earlier 'unbridled industry' about them; and the parts are drawn together by images of water, fish and animals, and word-echoes (gouge/garage; bronze/breathe; black/back).

Boston is a moral emblem, but also an objective fact: the subterranean garage is literally threatening both the Statehouse

20. In the dedication speech.

21. *F.U.D.*, p. 71.

Lowell talks of Lincoln in similar terms: 'For us and our country, he left Jefferson's ideals of freedom and equality joined to the Christian sacrificial act of death and rebirth'. *Lincoln and the Gettysburg Address*, ed. Allan Nevins, Urbana (University of Illinois) 1964, pp. 88–9.

and the monument. Anchored in the local and the historical, the whole drift of the poem, as of 'Jonathan Edwards in Western Massachusetts', is to make firm distinctions:

> Once my nose crawled like a snail on the glass;
> my hand tingled
> to burst the bubbles
> drifting from the noses of the cowed, compliant fish.
>
> My hand draws back.[22]

These lines offer a clue to the poem's achievement, and what distinguishes it from a conventional ode: Lowell recognises that the price of idealism, as Yeats discovered, is the turning of the heart to stone. The hunger for the sublime expresses at a deeper level that desire to master natural forces which ultimately turns to 'the lawlessness of something simple that has lost its law'. And so this most public of poems is also deeply personal: it shows, as does 'Middle Age', that the dinosaurs of unreason, the Leviathan, are both without and within, and answers to what George Steiner has referred to as: 'Freud's grim intimation of man's backward longing, of his covert wish for re-immersion in an earlier inarticulate state of organic existence'.[23]

Animals and statues, as Thomas Parkinson[24] has pointed out, are the two basic and complementary images of the whole book, marking the twin limits of man's ambivalent status in a fallen world. They come together in a group of poems—'Florence', 'July in Washington', 'The Neo-classical Urn', 'Caligula' and 'Buenos Aires'—distinguished by a compact vitality and a bizarre brilliance of invention. All are about the forces of idealism inherent in a civilisation's decay: the Judaic pull towards the

22. *F.U.D.*, p. 70.
In Pinter's *The Basement*, the fish tank, which is broken at the climax of the play, serves a similar function, as a symbol of contained animality, and the conflict in the play between the two men is a very Lowell-like one between Law and Stott ('stoat'). Another link between Pinter and this poem is the film, *The Servant*, for which Pinter wrote the script; its director, Joseph Losey, has said that it is about our society's servility.
23. *Language and Silence*, p. 56.
24. *Parkinson*, p. 145.

Law, the Roman drift towards politico-military tyranny, and the decline of imagination and intellect ('No/grace, no cerebration') in a violent and animalistic world.

In 'Florence', which uses phrases from Mary McCarthy's *The Stones of Florence*,[25] Lowell contrasts an unheroic contemporary Florence with the historical Florence of the child monster-killers represented in the statues of the Piazza—Perseus, David and Judith—and identifies with their victims, the monsters (the crabs, the 'formless', 'tubs of guts', 'chunks', 'slop'). 'July in Washington' sees the city as the centre of a world-wide power corruption which has retreated to a jungle state where statues 'ride like South American / liberators above the breeding vegetation'. In 'Buenos Aires', the unbending, stultifying world of these liberators is described:

> A false fin de siècle decorum
> snores over Buenos Aires[26]

Reacting against both the 'frogged coats' of the politicians and the 'starch-collars' of the crowds (both images of a neo-classic constriction imposed on the city), Lowell comes out on the side of life, as imaged in the 'bulky, beefy breathing of the herds'. The neo-classical properties are taken up in 'The Neo-Classical Urn'. The poem relates the balding adult Lowell to a childhood experience of turtle-catching, against a Boston background where even nature is trimmed to neo-classic proportions:

> . . . the colonnade
> of bleaching pines, cylindrical
> clipped trunks without a twig between them.[27]

The young Lowell of the poem behaved like the monster-killers and Melville's Ahab; now, as a man, he is the turtle, the survivor, and again, Lowell identifies with the 'monsters'. The poem's rhymes beautifully convey meaning, with the 'strummed'

25. *The Stones of Florence*, New York (Harcourt, Brace) 1959; London (Heinemann) 1963.
26. *F.U.D.*, p. 60.
27. *F.U.D.*, p. 47.

words of the elegy played off against the 'scummed' world of the turtles, and there is a neat progression of meanings in the half-rhymes of 'free will . . . kill . . . skull . . . shell'. 'Caligula', starting from Lowell's nickname (Cal), explicitly identifies the Roman emperor with the artist, both vainly trying to achieve the permanence of art. Caligula is that representative figure of the modern consciousness—the compound victim-and-agent—as is the Lowell of 'Middle Age' ('Father, forgive me / my injuries').

So many poems in *For the Union Dead* are ultimately about the terrifying isolation of the human condition. The alienation of a Caligula is one version; the anguished hyperaesthesia of the poet in the much-celebrated 'Night Sweat' is another:

> for ten nights now I've felt the creeping damp
> float over my pajamas' wilted white . . .[28]

'Night Sweat', 'Myopia: a Night', 'The Drinker' and 'Eye and Tooth' are poems which represent a fallen, secular world of despair, guilt and extreme self-torment, in which the anguish largely derives from the poet's inability to accept the kind of simplified relation with the outer world predicated in their very different ways by the early Puritans, Emerson, Whitman and William Carlos Williams. 'Fall 1961' focusses on one aspect of the problem. Like other poems in *For the Union Dead*, it is largely about the pressures of living in the void left by the withdrawal of transcendental bearings, with the decline of political and civic order, and in the consequent absence of moral sanctions. Individual security is a fiction, the poem says, when one is faced by the threat of nuclear war. But paradoxically, the poem denies both the security of words and of a consolatory, Wordsworthian attitude to nature's immutable processes, and yet proposes that there is indeed no other consolation but in words and nature. Human identity and community is defined in terms of the non-human, with a version of Jonathan Edwards' spider symbol:

> We are like a lot of wild
> spiders crying together
> but without tears.[29]

28. *F.U.D.*, p. 68. 29. *F.U.D.*, p. 11.

Even if a variation of the metaphor in 'The Flaw' suggests that human contact is yet more fragile than this—'Two walking cobwebs, almost bodiless, / crossed paths here once, kept house, and lay in beds'—the minimal experience of togetherness wins over a sense of sin, responsibility, and salvation, and the theological implications of the title are raised to be rejected: the 'fall' is the autumnal world of a planet on the edge of nuclear extinction. The measure of Lowell's progress from his pre-*Life Studies* days is the sustained control and meticulous, balanced exactness of the poem's structure, in which organic rhythms of the natural world play against the rhythms of the man-made world—prose, free verse and nursery rhyme. Thus, vision and logic cohere.

'It's as if no poet except Williams had really seen America or heard its language':[30] much of the particular distinctiveness of *For the Union Dead* is related to Lowell's awareness of the force of that tradition in American poetry which descends from Whitman to, variously, the Projectivists, the Beats, and most importantly, William Carlos Williams; it is a tradition which came to some prominence in American poetry in the 'sixties. The general relation of Lowell to Williams was discussed in the first chapter; in connection with *For the Union Dead*, it registers in a sense that, for Williams, there is an essential purity of the raw materials the poet works with. ('He really is utterly carried away into the object'.[31]) Yet, constantly throughout *For the Union Dead*, as several critics have pointed out, the poems propose for themselves sculptural and architectural metaphors; and the stone Lowell works with is impure, pregnant with history, guilt and morality. In two poems in particular—'The Mouth of the Hudson' and 'Eye and Tooth'—Lowell clarifies his relation to Williams beyond a doubt.

The 'single man' of 'The Mouth of the Hudson' seems a compound figure of various representatives of New England's past: the boy-naturalist, Jonathan Edwards; Thoreau, who 'named all the birds without a gun'; the Hawthorne who allegorised everything he saw; and Lowell himself ('Remember our lists of birds?'). But Lowell's persona in the poem has 'trouble with his balance':

30. Lowell, 'William Carlos Williams', in *Hudson Review*, XIV, Winter 1961, p. 534.
31. Alvarez interview in *The Review*, 8 August 1963, p. 38.

he looks upwards and downwards (perhaps at the double source of our torment in the spiritual and the natural) and cannot relate to the geographical dimension, that exploration of the wilderness, that merging and 'entering' of America which Whitmanite poetry invites. He remains firmly distinct from the landscape; for him, the ticking of the wild ice negates the eternal present of Whitmanite poetry, and the New Jersey industrial landscape, accepted by Williams, is seen as polluted to an unforgivable hell. 'Discarded ... condemned ... punctured': it reads like an epilogue to the American Dream. The poem's urban landscape, like those in 'Hawthorne', 'Returning' and 'Going to and fro', is simultaneously fact, allegory and inner psychological state.

For Williams' 'innocent eye',[32] Lowell substitutes an eye that is always committed, vulnerable and obsessive: the eye of memory, the myopic eye, the 'homicidal eye' of 'Man and Wife'; Hawthorne's 'disturbed eyes'; Major Myers' 'suffering almond eye'; or the 'glazed eye' of 'Returning'. In an early poem, Bernadette's vision of Our Lady 'put[s] out reason's eyes'; and we recall the limitations of Lowell's father's 'twenty-twenty' vision. In 'Eye and Tooth', Lowell uses material from his *Hudson Review* essay on Williams to describe both the physical agonies of a sore eye, and the way in which the poet's 'eye' of imagination shapes the poet's 'I' of personality: the poem works variations around this basic pun. 'An image of a white house with a blotch on it—this is perhaps the start of a Williams poem', Lowell says in his essay on Williams. But he teases this particular image into something very unlike Williams:

> I saw things darkly,
> as through an unwashed goldfish globe[33]

—the image is a favourite with Lowell, and recalls 'Fall 1961' and the title-poem. The poet's 'eye' brings up unpleasing

32. Kenneth Burke, 'The Methods of William Carlos Williams', in *Dial*, LXXXII, February 1927, pp. 94–8, says Williams 'is the master of the glimpse. There is the eye, and there is the thing upon which the eye alights; while the relationship existing between the two is the poem'.

33. *F.U.D.*, p. 18.

memories from the past which 'nothing can dislodge'; and yet, for Lowell, these memories are the fuel for poetry, 'a simmer of rot and renewal'. No balm can ease the pain, and with nothing to pour on those waters and flames which figure so importantly in the book, the poem ends:

> I am tired. Everyone's tired of my turmoil.[34]

It is a line which in its wintry discontent, its restlessness, is so very typical of the anguished Lowell of this book, and so very characteristically unheeding of Williams' advice in 'Paterson': 'Be reconciled, poet, with your world'.

Yet, in spite of the intensities, the style of 'Eye and Tooth' is compact and disciplined. For many readers it is this conjunction that is the main achievement of *For the Union Dead*; where many of the *Life Studies* poems were comparatively static, here we have a perpetual 'going to and fro', but the best poems convey a strong sense of selection and deliberation in terms of language and procedures, and a keen precision of observation. The poems' taut syntactical forms effectively process the often turbulent emotions. In places, the new energies are too 'stated'—in rhetorical questions, apostrophes, exclamations, a kind of indolent phrasing and throw-away endings; but in the best poems, there is a 'nervous alertness' (Dickey[35]), a 'shimmer' (Cosgrave,[36] Alvarez[37]).One is reminded of the last line in 'Soft Wood': 'Each drug that numbs alerts another nerve to pain'—the apparently 'cool' style often works in that way; or, using metaphors from another poem, one can say that these poems are both statuesque and breathing, and they have 'an angry wrenlike vigilance, a greyhound's gentle tautness'.

For the Union Dead therefore proves that nagging doubts about *Life Studies*—that too much of the essential 'meat' of poetry might have been sacrificed in the process of divesting the early poetry's

---

34. *F.U.D.*, p. 19.

35. William Dickey, 'Poetic Language', in *Hudson Review*, XVII, 1964–65, p. 595.

36. Patrick Cosgrave, *The Public Poetry of Robert Lowell*, London (Gollancz) 1970, p. 162.

37. A. Alvarez, review of *F.U.D.*, in *The Observer*, 14 March 1965, p. 26.

rhetoric—were unfounded. In some ways, *For the Union Dead* subsumes *Life Studies* into its constant commentary on the past. The book points in four directions: there are the personal poems about a relationship of love and marriage; poems about an unhappy childhood; poems which take the exposure of the tormented self further than ever before, and make this the most Baudelairean of Lowell's books; and poems in which Lowell has gone beyond a limited 'confessional' mode, and an interest in New World innocence, and come through to a truly public poetry, of which the finest flowering is the title-poem. The book offers the possibility of a public poetry which doesn't aim to persuade or argue, as traditional public poetry often does, but to alert and sensitise the reader; and one based on the primacy of the material world and constantly drawing on the creative/destructive potential in the cyclic processes of civilisation's and nature's 'rot and renewal'—something taken up in the next book. Throughout *For the Union Dead*, there is a constant returning to the landscapes—mental, moral and aesthetic—of Lowell's earlier poetry; at the same time, there is a widened historical and topographical interest—to the Classical world (another foretaste of the next book) and to Florence, South America, etc. All this enforces a sense of common humanity, which is perhaps the strongest thing to emerge from the book, particularly in 'Jonathan Edwards in Western Massachusetts', 'Fall 1961' and the marriage poems; and there is both candour towards oneself, and compassion towards others, in the portrayals of failure, guilt, loss and physical pain—something rarely apparent in the 'forties Lowell but establishing itself in *Life Studies*. Lowell has earned his 'survivor's smile'.

6 Our Monotonous Sublime

In a Note to the next book, *Near the Ocean* (1967), Lowell allowed himself a touch of arch bemusement: 'How one jumps from Rome to the America of my own poems is something of a mystery to me.' No follower of Lowell's career up to 1967 could honestly claim a dearth of clues and need the hint that it was Sidney Nolan's charcoal drawings that made the transfer, for had not the poet been sign-posting the 'roads and sewers'[1] back to the city of Pope and Caesar for years in such a variety of poems as 'Dea Roma', 'Falling Asleep over the Aeneid', 'Beyond the Alps', 'For George Santayana' and 'Caligula'? And no reader was likely to forget that, more than twenty years before, Lowell had made his pilgrimage to Rome, and written of a contemporary Boston where the 'trollop' danced on the founders' skulls.[2] With *Near the Ocean*, the reader's problem was how to account for another jump: from Lowell's participation in the Pentagon March of October 1967—his deepest political commitment since his 'fire-breathing Catholic C.O.'[3] days—to poems which seemed to mark a return to an urbanity and classicism quite out of key with contemporary radical pieties. The unusual thinness of the book, even with Nolan's drawings to fulflesh the American editions, seemed to stand for the slim survival in modern poetry of 'the fragile, sacred seed / of ancient Roman virtue', as one of the new poems puts it; less reverently, it had the air of a thin-lipped cultural regression before the 'sixties horde of beat-ified poetic redskins. 'These strange new poems'; 'this odd new clutch of texts'[4]—these fairly represent the critics' initial puzzlement.

1. *P.*, p. 60.   2. *P.*, p. 67.   3. *L.S.*, p. 99.
4. Respectively, Hayden Carruth, 'A Meaning of Robert Lowell', in *Hudson Review*, XX, Autumn 1967, p. 430; Richard Howard, 'Fuel on the Fire', in *Poetry*, CX, 1967, p. 413.

For the Union Dead had offered more than a hint of the neo-classicism to come, with its properties of bronze and marble, of urns and symmetrically-constructed cities; and the American landscape with its monuments, buildings and place-names fills in the rest. Not surprisingly, some of the book's early readers saw this newest Lowell as a modern Arnold, or as the latter-day Vergil of America that Ransom once predicted he might become; others saw a reader of the entrails, and Cyril Connolly settled for a perfection of 'gravel-voiced despair'.[5] Yet there is in the book's vision of a cooling planet, and in its air of troubled stoicism, a strenuous commitment to contemporary living, and it is with a 'complicatedly civilised'[6] view of culture that Lowell drills deep to expose the nerve-ends of our civilisation which he places in its death-wished 'jungle hour' and 'near the ocean' of some final dissolution. Water is the basic symbol and the common creative/destructive element; ancient Mediterranean and modern Atlantic are as one, 'can only speak the present tense', and unlike 'older seas', give no asylum; and 'nearness' to the ocean, not 'merging' or 'immersion', is civilised humanity's condition.

The ocean of the title also points the stark impermanence of stone and marble: beyond the monuments of history are its ruins; beyond its ruins, only deserts. (This reminds us that another version of the Lambkin story of man's ingratitude tells how Poseidon, the sea-monster, built the walls of Troy, and was similarly unrewarded.) The poems themselves seem like sur-viving monuments dedicated to a former grandeur; in a pitching for the high style, all the properties of rhetoric are laid out—paradoxes, puns, antitheses, archaisms, apostrophes and literary allusions. And yet these 'monuments' are subject to a restless flux, contain tremendous energies, are nothing like the 'stiff quatrains shovelled out four-square' referred to in the opening poem. The old rhetorical devices have re-appeared in new sur-roundings, with the short-breathed cadences of *For the Union Dead* subsumed into the larger metres of an eight-line stanza of four-foot couplets. Basically, this is Marvell's famous stanza, and one that Lowell had once rejected as being too 'regular' and rhetorical

5. Cyril Connolly, in *Sunday Times*, 2 July 1967, p. 27.
6. Alvarez interview, in *The Review*, 8, August 1963, p. 40.

for his purposes;[7] now, in *Near the Ocean*, he finds a new use for a form in which the artifice seems to generate an inner tension, what Yeats once called 'a passionate syntax for passionate subject-matter'. Each of the book's three major poems—'Waking Early Sunday Morning', 'Fourth of July in Maine' and 'Near the Ocean'—is essentially a lyric monologue which uses Marvell's line in dissimilar ways, and to very different ends.

'Waking Early Sunday Morning' is the most rewarding of the three, though it has received some over-enthusiastic praise from critics mistaking what is a very ambitious intention for the deed.[8] A poem with both a positive and negative urge, it celebrates 'the potentiality of man to achieve moral order'[9] but is also a tragic facing of the limitations of the world modern man has created, 'an elegy mourning a sterile world without God or gods'.[10] It uses a wide range of aspects of the American Dream, from the time of the Pilgrim Fathers to the present day, as a narrative thread to link the random thoughts of the poem's subject: a combined figure of a universal Sunday American for whom the rituals of 'spire and flagpole' are drained of meaning, and Lowell himself, still haunted by dreams of America's lost innocence and tormented by its oppressive Calvinism. In the poem's fifth stanza, the protagonist slowly regains consciousness and sees:

> . . . a glass of water wet
> with a fine fuzz of icy sweat,
> silvery colours touched with sky,
> serene in their neutrality.[11]

7. *P.R.*, pp. 246–7.

8. Thus, Michael London, in *London and Boyers*, says, 'If the projective-proselytes, the starvelings weaned on Charles Olson, fail to respond to this poem, offer them milk for dehydrated lines and honey for hemorrhoidal words; then lead these crusading emasculators of the American idiom, manipulators of the low-moan, breathtaking asthmatics, chickenshit disclaimers, erudite dabblers, pipsqueak poetasters, from the page to the privy and let them be', p. 102; and Patrick Cosgrave, in *The Public Poetry of Robert Lowell*, p. 203, 'It has no internal flaws'.

9. Patrick Cosgrave, *The Public Poetry of Robert Lowell*, p. 197.

10. Hilda Link, 'A Tempered Triumph', in *Prairie Schooner*, XLI, 1967–68, p. 440.

11. *N.O.*, p. 14.

A moment of calm—delicately enacted in the soft consonants—conveys a kind of pristine joy in the moral neutrality of the natural world; but the mood is impossible to prolong, and the objects become invested with the kind of sombre symbolic significance Lowell's poetry constantly draws towards:

> yet if I shift, or change my mood,
> I see some object made of wood,
> background behind it of brown grain,
> to darken it, but not to stain[12]

—a reminder, if we needed one, that this is a Sunday awakening. The heroic burden of our human consciousness—whether that of a Lowell, or the President Johnson who appears in a later stanza —is to feel the compulsion to use our energies to impose an order on the world, and yet to see this ordering issue in a constant limitation of our personal freedoms, as the dream of democratic liberties which inspired the state's founders is now lost in 'open sores, / fresh breakage, fresh promotions, chance / assassinations, no advance'. These phrases suggest how very much this poem is in touch with the dilemmas of American political life in the 'sixties.

The central section of the poem ranges across a basic trinity of all civilisations, in the church, trade and the military—important aspects of the order and energies that man displays. There is a rich display of puns, colloquialisms used savagely and ironically, allusions, sudden switches of perspective, all-pervasive images of light and dark, and of wood. Typical is the following stanza which, coming at the climax of the poem, takes off from the previous stanza's last word ('mad') and presents a hollow, echoing world of Philistine-Roman-Carthaginian militarism, with Vietnam as the contemporary experience giving pressure to the lines:

> Hammering military splendor,
> top-heavy Goliath in full armor—
> little redemption in the mass
> liquidations of their brass,

12. *N.O.*, p. 14.

> elephant and phalanx moving
> with the times and still improving,
> when that kingdom hit the crash:
> a million foreskins stacked like trash . . .[13]

Although the clanging stresses are reminiscent of Lowell's earlier poetry, the kinæsthetic effects, and the rhymes, rhythms and word-play are used for more precisely-defined and controlled purposes than before. For example, there is the parody of the Puritan-capitalist work-ethic in: 'redemption . . . liquidations'; 'mass . . . brass'; and 'improving'. 'Mass / liquidations of the brass' also slangily suggests killings ordered by the American military establishment (brass-hats), the biblical 'sounding-brass', and liquid stock. The last line, referring to an Old Testament story of mass slaughter, echoes backwards to the 'stacked birch' of a previous stanza, and forwards to the Juvenal of the *Tenth Satire* in tone. The bristling sarcasm in this stanza seems to have derived from Pound's corrosive style, joined to a type of savage, bludgeoning declamation found in some early Puritan writers.

The nub of the poem is in two lyric cries—'O to break loose'; 'anywhere, but somewhere else!'—which convey a Promethean sense both of man's limitless energies and a despairing recognition of the inevitable corroding of individual aspirations. The universal anguish of free will is caught in this picture of President Johnson in the posture of an overburdened Roman emperor:

> O to break loose. All life's grandeur
> is something with a girl in summer . . .
> elated as the President
> girdled by his establishment
> this Sunday morning, free to chaff
> his own thoughts with his bear-cuffed staff,
> swimming nude, unbuttoned, sick
> of his ghost-written rhetoric![14]

The stanza relates everything that the poem has so far said to a general view of contemporary national life.

13. *N.O.*, p. 15.
14. *N.O.*, p. 16.

The poem concludes with a kind of Audenesque general compassion:

> Pity the planet, all joy gone
> from this sweet volcanic cone;
> peace to our children when they fall
> in small war on the heels of small
> war—until the end of time
> to police the earth, a ghost
> orbiting forever lost
> in our monotonous sublime.[15]

The ghosts of the past, as well as the Holy Ghost, haunt Lowell's America, and the ghost of a future dead planet. This ending is the most successful part of a poem which reflects a complex of contradictions without quite deploying them in a controlled way —discipline and freedom; free will and determinism; hero and victim; instinctive forces and those of the rational life. (In these stresses, the poem does mirror very accurately one crucial confrontation of American public life in the 'sixties: that of a rational, but debilitated public spirit and older liberalism with a new radical, more heroic consciousness which, like so many in American history, has abandoned moderation.) 'Waking Early Sunday Morning' is a public poem but, lacking that inward authority which Yeats' mature poetry assumes, Lowell uses a wide range of 'borrowings' of other writers' styles and themes— there are echoes of Homer, Marvell, Arnold, Emerson, Hopkins, Baudelaire, Yeats, Stevens, Eliot and Betjeman—as an inducement to persuade the reader to follow him in his modulations, from despair to a nervous kind of exaltation. But the 'poetry' and the 'rhetoric', in Yeats' terms, cut loose from each other, and Lowell's instincts force him continually to say things with an obliquity that never marries well with the straightforward assertion of other parts. Marvell's lines have a sharpness and precision that Lowell's lack at crucial moments, and the general failure to achieve an assured articulation suggests a contemporary of Marvell, Cowley, and even, in places, Emerson:

15. *N.O.*, p. 16.

Lowell admires what he calls 'the conscious, urbane exaggeration'[16] of the latter's 'Concord Hymn'.

Too much in 'Waking Early Sunday Morning', and in *Near the Ocean* as a whole, finally depends upon what meaning the reader can inject into the phrase 'monotonous sublime'[17]—a phrase with both Baudelairean and classical connotations. Perhaps it is expected to convey too much: a tragic loss of palpability, reality devolved into fiction, the reduction of the world to a reverberating 'hollow cone', America's hunger to be major in everything and to shape life to grandiose notions, and a peculiarly American mixture of Life and Art, where 'the artist's existence becomes his art . . . he hardly exists without it . . . and almost sheds his other life'.[18] Lowell's difficulties in finding a single focus to convey adequately the sense of being an artist in contemporary America are pointed by a remark in the Naipaul interview: 'America with a capital A I find a very hard thing to realise. It's beyond any country, it's an empire'[19] hence, the imperial theme running through *Near the Ocean*. But a 'mistranslation' in one of the book's Quevedo sonnets—*patria* transmogrified to *casa*—points the reader in another direction, towards that white Colonial frame house ('the Americas' / best artifact produced en masse') which 'Fourth of July in Maine', another in the long line of Lowell poems about celebratory dates, offers as an emblem of an alternative, less transcendent view of sublimity. A person's possessions define him, and in this poem, the house and its furniture propose a 'softer wood' answer to that 'longing after the bliss of the commonplace' which Mann's *Tonio Kröger*[20] suggests is characteristic of the true artist.

16. Interview with John McCormick, 'Falling Asleep over Grillparzer', in *Poetry*, LXXXI, January 1953, p. 275.
17. The word 'monotonous' occurs frequently in Lowell's work. Thus:
>'nature's monotonous backlash' *F.U.D.*, p. 24.
>'the monotonous frontier' *N.*, p. 28.
>'The world's monotonous and small' *I.*, p. 71.
>'Real life is a simple monotonous thing' *O.G.*, p. 150.
18. *Alvarez*, p. 43.
19. *Naipaul*, p. 302.
20. *Tonio Kröger*, London (Dent: Everyman) 1940, p. 68: 'there is a way of being an artist that goes so deep and is so much a matter of origins and destinies that no longing seems to it sweeter and more worth knowing than longing after the bliss of the commonplace'.

The poem is about two kinds of 'innocence': one is that
enshrined in America's national identity, from the naive faith of
the state's founders, via Emersonian Transcendentalism, to the
uncomplicated politics of a contemporary Independence Day
parade; the other is that of children, the instinctive world of
animals ('harmonies / of lust and appetite and ease'), a pre-Fall
Eden world ('that time of gentleness'), and supremely, that
represented by the poet's older cousin, Harriet Winslow. After
years of poetic scourings of his family's past, Lowell now celebrates
in this woman and her former Castine house the coming together
of the New England qualities of proportion, purpose, decorum,
and the Horatian virtues of 'friends, independence, and a house'.
Atlantic meets Mediterranean.

The Harriet Winslow house is a repository of the best of the
early American values but, under its present owners, it has declined into a symbolic shell, a 'hollow cone', for the garden is
decayed, and the inside is disordered:

> And now the frosted summer night-dew
> brightens, the north wind rushes through
> your ailing cedars, finds the gaps;
> thumbtacks rattle from the white maps,
> food's lost sight of, dinner waits,
> in the cold oven, icy plates—
> repeating and repeating, one
> Joan Baez on the gramophone.
>
> And here in your converted barn,
> we burn our hands a moment, borne
> by energies that never tire
> of piling fuel on the fire;
> monologue that will not hear,
> logic turning its deaf ear,
> wild spirits and old sores in league
> with inexhaustible fatigue[21]

—this last phrase, like 'monotonous sublime' and with an equally
Baudelairean ring, sums up the particular energies of *Near the*

21. *N.O.*, pp. 20–1.

Ocean. Lowell, a poet of restlessness without repose, has caught that deep-seated uncertainty and emptiness at the centre of the modern consciousness: the nervous gestures which hide a spiritual exhaustion, the clinging to an extraneous warmth because of an inner chill. In these two stanzas is the 'heart' of this often elusive book, the nearest it approaches to the 'feel' of twentieth-century living. The converted barn, the cedars, the thumbtacks, a record by Joan Baez, whose protest songs point the lost harmonies of a world vacated, like the Winslow house, by its previous owner —the details have a logic of thought and feeling rare in *Near the Ocean*.

The main images—the blueness of innocence and mortality, hot and cold, and music—are finely ordered; but what particularly stays in the mind is the poem's grace and humour, with Marvell's voice and stanza adapted to witty and gently-ironic musings:

> gone, as the Christians say, for good.

> Her two angora guinea pigs
> are nibbling seed, the news, and twigs[22]

Finally, there is in the picture of Harriet a moment of calm at the symbolic centre of the book's turbulent energies. Throughout Lowell's account of the often tragic details of her life, the accents are those of the *Life Studies* poem on Santayana, who died 'unbelieving, unconfessed and unreceived', and yet, like Harriet, stood for a saving grace, proportion and endurance. To re-phrase an earlier line: 'The world shall come to Castine': at a time when the power- and success-gods are worshipped, world-losers such as the Brunetto Latini, Brutus, Dante and Harriet Winslow of this book can help us to recover, in the self and in civilisation, a primal 'ceremony of innocence'. For the poet, it is also something to correct that 'self-conscious . . . mandarin "seriousness"' [23] which Alfred Appel Jr. sees as the American literary intellectuals'

22. *N.O.*, pp. 18 and 20, respectively.
23. Alfred Appel Jr., in *Nabokov: Criticism, reminiscences, translations and tributes*, ed. Alfred Appel Jr. and Charles Newman, Evanston (Northwestern Press) 1970; London (Weidenfeld & Nicolson) 1971, p. 26.

legacy from Henry James, and from which *Near the Ocean* is not wholly free.

But it is a precarious achievement. 'I am a worshipper of myth and monster':[24] historical meets psychological discontinuity in the title-poem, where Lowell takes up the theme of 'Florence' in *For the Union Dead*, and presents monster- and tyrant-killing as another aspect of America's 'leap for the sublime'.[25] The least public, the most personal and interiorised of the trio of major poems, 'Near the Ocean' is also the most difficult. Lowell rings further changes on the possibilities of the Marvellian stanza, and here it is both more clotted and more harrowing, ranging from the Websterian to the Baudelairean, and with something of the compressed rhetoric of parts of Hopkins, but with a modernistic use of disjointed images and montage-like effects. Relating the decline of a marriage to that of a civilisation, it is Lowell's Waste Land, and presents images of betrayal, sterility, drought and violent sexuality against a background of two elliptically-treated classical myths of, respectively, monsters and betrayal: Perseus and the Gorgon, and the Clytemnestra-Aegisthus-Orestes story.

Although it later transforms itself into a tender, moving tribute to a woman, the poem begins on very much the 'horror' side of the greatness-cum-horror syndrome Lowell mentions in his 'Note' to the book, with the public beheading of a Medusa figure:

> The house is filled. The last heartthrob
> thrills through her flesh. The hero stands,
> stunned by the applauding hands,
> and lifts her head to please the mob . . .[26]

Lowell neatly condenses sex- and death-themes in the pun of 'heartthrob', and there is an 'erotic terror' trill in the alliteration of the first two lines. The heroic idealism that the Classical world has bequeathed to the twentieth century is pictured here as a stage performance for a mob. The next episode is a confrontation of a brother and sister (Orestes and Electra?) with their mother,

24. *N.*, p. 82.
25. *Alvarez*, p. 42.
26. *N.O.*, p. 25.

a Clytemnestra figure of power ('iron-bruises') and sexuality ('powder'), who seems a nightmare version of the mother of '91 Revere Street'.[27] But the hero rejects the destruction of this second woman of the poem, who fuses with the Medusa of the opening, because it would be a total capitulation to violence. Then, moving into modern times, the second part of the poem traces the history of a marriage in terms of physical surroundings; water plays a prominent part, and imagery evoking successive stages of American history, from a 'black and white inland New England back-drop', through the period of industrial growth, to the nadir of the Depression and urban squalor.

The epilogue has the accents of a convinced gravity:

> Sleep, sleep. The ocean, grinding stones,
> can only speak the present tense;
> nothing will age, nothing will last,
> or take corruption from the past.
> A hand, your hand then! I'm afraid
> to touch the crisp hair on your head—
> Monster loved for what you are,
> till time, that buries us, lay bare[28]

—we return to the sleep with which the book began. The contemporary woman of the poem's second part is now explicitly identified with the Medusa-monster/Clytemnestra mother of the opening. The point that Lowell seems to be making is that to accept the monster in others is to accept the monsters in oneself, and that this is where both humanity and creativity start; the artist, in working in the area of the satanic and the monstrous, recognises some occult link between these and creation. At the end of the poem, the hero moves with the ebb and flow of civilisations in a coming to terms with Time and the ocean's monotonous cyclic creative-and-destructive processes, and life in 'the present tense', the terms of our human condition.

27. Richard J. Fein, in *Robert Lowell*, p. 145, says of the women in Lowell's poetry: '[They] tend to be forces that go beyond the comprehension and the control of the men in the poems.'

28. *N.O.*, p. 27.

'Near the Ocean' is an intensely personal poem, but it also touches on the dark underside of civilisation, a world of public squalors and private fears, some other side of the coin to the eternal monotonous sublimities. These quotidian terrors are also very much in evidence in the remaining poems of the title-sequence—'The Opposite House' and 'Central Park'. Both poems have affinities with some of Juvenal's in their deployment of human artifacts: an abandoned house and a sordid urban park are part of an updated Audenesque landscape of fear and crisis. An 'opposite' image to the Harriet Winslow house, the house of the first poem is square, rectilinear, and marooned both from human society and the consolations of memory; in some ways, the poem seems to enact the class, racial and historical ambivalencies surrounding the Revere Street house: 'even in the palmy, *laissez-faire* '20's, Revere Street refused to be a straightforward, immutable residential fact. From one end to the other, houses kept being sanded down, repainted, or abandoned to the flaking of decay. Houses, changing hands, changed their language and nationality.' Only the poet's imagination can recreate 'its manly, old-fashioned lines', and in its decline it has become ornate, foreign, as unreal and remote as heraldry. The baroque crudities of our civilisation feature, too, in 'Central Park' in the poem's 'silver foil', 'gold leaf' and embalming rituals. The park's decline recalls that of Boston's Common and Public Garden in Lowell's early work, and in the title-poem of *For the Union Dead*. Jail, jungle, lost childhood Eden—the pervasive human–animal analogies suggest drugged helplessness, mindless violence, and sordid sexuality, with, unlike Albee's 'Zoo Story', no redemptive possibilities.

'The Opposite House' and 'Central Park' are minor, impressionistic poems, but they exhibit the very faults which partly disfigure the major poems of *Near the Ocean*. There is something mannered about the lines, as in the overtly metaphysical tenor of

> one figure of geometry,
> multiplied to infinity,

('Central Park')[29]

29. *N.O.*, p. 23.

and the voyeuristic eye leads to an arbitrariness and staginess of effects, a vamping up in the tradition of the American Gothic:

> Drugged and humbled by the smell
> of zoo-straw mixed with animal,
> the lion prowled his slummy cell,
> serving his life-term in jail—
> glaring, grinding, on his heel,
> with tingling step and testicle . . .
>
> ('Central Park')[30]

—the nervous menace, the edginess, the obsessive rhymes have a bland, unearned quality about them. When the poetry of this book is bad, it is usually in the way that Lowell's translation of *Phèdre* is bad: melodramatic, frenetic, hopped-up. Cleanth Brooks maybe right in seeing the 'stark confrontation'[31] as the distinctively new and vital element in modern poetry, but one ought perhaps to recognise its limitations as a poetic method when used without a quite old-fashioned sense of decorum.

The 'stark confrontation' of past and present everywhere in *Near the Ocean* is perhaps a less disturbing feature of Lowell's post-Eliot lineage. But if Lowell is committed to the twentieth century in a way that Eliot never was ('For all the horrors of this age, and for all the attractions of others . . . I'd rather be alive now than at any other time I know of. This age is mine, and I want very much to be a part of it.'[32]), he has to an almost classic degree what George Steiner calls an 'hunger for precedents', and his translations in the book's second half answer this peculiarly American urge. In explicitly calling them 'translations' rather than 'imitations', Lowell seems to be implying that their function is more to offer a kind of historical sheet-anchor, than to re-create a classical world directly into twentieth-century terms: filling out the 'Roman' decadence of contemporary America, they posit a 'timeless present' in which 'electric church bells' and the barbaric splendours of Carthage are viewed simultaneously in a kind of 'cubist' perspective.

30. *N.O.*, p. 23.

31. 'Poetry since "The Waste Land"', in *Southern Review*, I, No. 3, Summer 1965, pp. 487–500.

32. Quoted in Jay Martin, *Robert Lowell*, p. 5.

In spite of the fact that he read Classics at Kenyon, the desire to re-create something of the Latin poets' atmosphere in his own poetry seems to have come late to Lowell; as he constantly stresses their 'maturity', it was perhaps a conscious decision to reserve them for his own poetic maturity? He has emphasised[33] how much more 'modern' the Latin authors are than the Greek, in their particular complex of dualities: passion and coldness; sophistication and rawness; realism and formality. Something like these qualities comes across in these two lines from Lowell's own 'Caligula'—

> You stare down hallways, mile on stoney mile,
> where statues of the gods return your smile[34]

—and no doubt he was trying to achieve the Latin poets' virtues in the original poems of *Near the Ocean*. In the book's second half, the catalyst that releases Lowell's imagination is Horace's poetry —even to the point where the accurate transference of the original is a comparatively secondary matter. (Thus, 'polished goblets' and 'capacious shells' become, respectively, 'frail' and 'fragile'.) Lowell sharpens the merely hinted effects of the originals, replacing neutral words by more nervous ones, and alternatively, reduces pleasantly-evocative words and phrases to something flat and bare. His version of Horace's 'Spring Ode' opens: 'Sharp winter melts and changes into spring— / now the west wind, now cables haul the boats / on their dry hulls . . . .' The original's welcoming address to the new season has been rough-edged, as if we are now on the Atlantic seaboard at the end of a New England winter, rather than by the Mediterranean, and in the heightened air of desolation, the lines lose some of Horace's proportion and dignity. Yet in spite of the freedom Lowell has allowed himself, these versions are better as poems than those of two representative translators, Helen Rowe Henze[35] and James Michie.[36] One brief comparison will have to suffice: Lowell's

33. *P.R.*, pp. 255–7.
34. *F.U.D.*, p. 49.
35. Helen Rowe Henze, *The Odes of Horace*, Norman (University of Oklahoma Press) 1961.
36. James Michie, *The Odes of Horace*, London (Hart-Davis) 1964.

'the brief sum of life forbids / our opening any long account
with hope' surely wins over Henze's limp 'Life's so brief span
thus forbids us to undertake hopes that stretch out too long' and
the clumsiness of Michie's 'Life's brief tenure forbids high hopes
to be built in disproportion'? Henze's versions, in particular,
show how inadequate English translations are that attempt to
follow the original metres, incapable of the rhythmically-exciting
breathlessness of Lowell's 'Cleopatra' Ode:

> O Cleopatra, scarcely escaping,
>
> and with a single ship, and scarcely
> escaping from your limping fleet, on fire,
> Cleopatra, with Caesar running on the wind,
> three rising stands of oars, with Caesar
>
> falling on you like a sparrow hawk
> fallen on some soft dove or sprinting rabbit
> in the winter field.[37]

In some ways, a translator's difficulties are increased if he
takes a classic popular with translators. In the case of Juvenal's
Tenth Satire, there is always the lively ghost of Johnson's version
to be laid. If we compare the openings of Johnson's and Lowell's
versions, Johnson's lines are seen to come through with a pressure
derived from the depth of the poet's experience, from a long
tradition of Christian stoicism, and from his sense of representing
a consensus of opinion to society. Faithful as Lowell's opening is
to the original, it is unexciting. Lowell does, throughout his
version, hit the darkly-pessimistic tone and impact of Juvenal,
but it is a Juvenal coarsened by harsh rhythms and gratuitous
crudities:

> . . . the cuckold chops the lover's
> balls off, or jams a mullet up his arse.[38]
>
> . . . his swelling prick—sad sacks in heat,
> their conscience washing out between their legs.[39]

37. *N.O.*, p. 33.   38. *N.O.*, p. 46.   39. *N.O.*, p. 46.

The original's pagan indecencies are rendered down to graffiti. Yet comparison of Lowell's version to Johnson's is unfair, for it is nearer to a translation in Dryden's vein than to a free-ranging 'imitation', and keeps quite close to the original, in spite of individual omissions and condensations, and the heightened contemporaneity. For more extended comparison of different versions of Juvenal, one could take lines 47–66 in Dryden's version ('Democritus could feed his spleen . . .') and the equivalent passage in Lowell, beginning 'Democritus could laugh till he was sick . . . '. What Lowell's version so damagingly lacks is a sense of 'the foppish gravity of show':

> while, with dumb pride, and a set formal face,
> He moves in the dull ceremonial track
>
> (Dryden).[40]

Though without Johnson's gravity, Dryden speaks to and on behalf of his neo-classic age, and pride, form, ceremony mean something that gives due force to the criticism implied in 'dumb' and 'dull'. The details of the Lowell carry little of this kind of wider resonance, and his lines lack the formal impetus of either heroic couplets or eight-line octosyllabic stanzas. Strangely, it is Dryden who, for his time, has the more contemporary ring of the two.

Rendering Juvenal demands an intensity of creation, with objects and people made vivid and assailed from a position of moral superiority, and the miracle of Johnson's version is the sense of violent energies tempered by the language. Without the moral status, Lowell lacks assurances of language and form; the neo-classic urge that prompted these translations offers no viable, unified style. Perhaps the main consolation for the reader is that Lowell's Romans sometimes come across with a physical impact reminiscent of Ben Jonson's. But what happens when Lowell cuts his losses and operates simply as an academic translator rendering an original as faithfully as possible is shown by

40. *The Poems of Dryden*, ed. George R. Noyes, Boston (Houghton, Mifflin) 1950, p. 348.

his version of Canto XV of Dante's *Inferno*.[41] Though free from the excesses of parts of the other translations, it never rises much above a low plateau of ordinariness. The withering away of civilised standards in thirteenth-century Florence is its theme, and Brunetto Latini is one of the stoic heroes of this very stoic book, something of a Santayana. Like Dante, Lowell sees himself as an exile from his native city and in search of civic order. A more lugubrious version of the city-theme is offered by 'The Ruins of Time'—a sonnet-sequence of four poems from the Spanish of Quevedo and Gongora; the freest translations of the book, these are yet remarkably successful as poems in their own right.

In these final poems, Rome and Carthage emerge as joint symbols of the decline of civilisations. But we also hear an echo of the book's earlier emblematic 'white Colonial frame house':

> I saw the musty shingles of my house,
> raw wood and fixed once, now a wash of moss
> eroded by the ruins of the age.[42]

Atlantic and Mediterranean meet again in this image of a decayed house. Finally, Rome, like Boston with its ditch, 'has fallen in its grave'. The lesson offered contemporary America is that sham glories inevitably corrode into debilitating uncertainties—'what was firm has fled. What once / was fugitive maintains its permanence'.

The 'cooling meteorite' of the book's closing lines recalls the endings of the book's first two poems, and also proposes an image

---

41. In 'Tradition and the Individual Talent', Eliot uses Canto XV as an illustration in an argument about the transmuting of feelings into art: 'Canto XV of the *Inferno* [Brunetto Latini] is a working up of the emotion evident in the situation; but the effect, though single as that of any work of art, is obtained by considerable complexity of detail. The last quatrain gives an image, a feeling attaching to an image, which "came", which did not develop simply out of what precedes, but which was probably in suspension in the poet's mind until the proper combination arrived for it to add itself to.' (*Selected Essays*, London (Faber) 1932, pp. 18–19.) Readers of Lowell's poetry, from *Life Studies* onwards, might be struck with the aptness of the passage as a description of Lowell's own poetic practice.

42. *N.O.*, p. 53.

for this latest Lowell; still very much a divided man, he is pulled in contrary directions by stasis and energy, pity and despair, gentleness and anger. A generalised pathos, an engraved, marmoreal pessimism substitute uneasily in *Near the Ocean* for that pity towards individuals and that involvement in a common humanity of *For the Union Dead*; and the greater urbanity goes with a loss of the previous book's poised incisiveness. In spite of the distancing effect of working through Marvell and Horace, the poems overplay the Steinerian agonies of a 'post-culture'[43] and the mordant critique of our present discontents. The nagging feeling persists that, as Diana Trilling[44] found in *Who's Afraid of Virginia Woolf?* (significantly set in New Carthage), a vein of self-indulgence runs through Lowell's Night Thoughts on American life, and a priming of the reader's stock responses to the 'boredom, and the horror, and the glory'. Is *Near the Ocean* a kind of Harvard horror of the simple response, or an effort to temper despairing energies in the integrity of a style, some 'cool web' of language?

Throughout *Near the Ocean*, the force of Lowell's imagination seems about to spin out of control; yet if, as G. S. Fraser says, 'True poets are people ready to ruin themselves',[45] the reader will make allowances. Again, Lowell has attempted to remake himself. A special debt to William Carlos Williams was acknowledged in *For the Union Dead*, but for a poet whose poetic geography lies elsewhere than in his country's raw natural and urban solitudes—New England, the South, Europe—the assimilation of Williams could only be a stage to something less idiosyncratically American. *Near the Ocean* is in the tradition of Vergil, Dante, Baudelaire and Eliot, staking all on a belief in the autonomy of the poem, and of the culture it is a part of. 'Sand, / Atlantic ocean, condoms, sand'—in the stating there is a kind of stay against the forces of fragmentation in American poetry, and in American life generally, in the 'sixties.

43. See George Steiner, 'In a post-culture', in *Extra-Territorial*, New York (Atheneum) 1970; London (Faber) 1972.

44. Diana Trilling, *Claremont Essays*, New York (Harcourt, Brace) 1964.

45. G. S. Fraser, *Ezra Pound*, Edinburgh (Oliver & Boyd) 1960, p. 81.

7   Blue Skies and Charred Carbons

In 1967, Lowell contributed to a *Partisan Review* symposium of American artists and intellectuals on 'What's happening to America'. His replies to a series of questions on the White House incumbency, inflation, poverty, the split between the Administration and the intellectuals, the Civil Rights issue, and American foreign policy are predictably gloomy. Only in his answers to the symposium's last two questions—about America's future—does anything like a glimmer of qualified optimism break through:

> I have a gloomy premonition . . . that we will soon
> look back on this troubled moment as a golden time
> of freedom and licence to act and speculate. One
> feels the steely sinews of the tiger, an ascetic, 'moral'
> and authoritarian reign of piety and iron.
>
> Doom or promise must be found in youth. I think
> perhaps the young hope for things that neither we nor
> any previous generation dared hope for. But how much
> like us, and what a slender reed, they often seem![1]

Both predictions came true in the year when they were made—perhaps the last year of political innocence in American life. Doom or promise: as with Yeats fifty years before, a 'terrible beauty' was born in a plague year of assassinations, urban violence, and conflicts that deeply divided the nation. Pushed by concerns that demanded more than the refusal of a White House invitation, Lowell participated in the Pentagon March, and set about producing his most ambitious and politically-motivated book to date.

1. *Partisan Review*, XXXIV, 1967, p. 38.

The book's changes of title, before it finally settled down to a career as *Notebook*, suggest the way it straddles an area covered by history, myth and autobiography. It began life as *Notebook of a Year*,[2] which befits the cyclic and seasonal myths which provide a large measure of its structure. Then, in its first edition, it appeared as *Notebook 1967-1968*, which reads like an attempt to match Mailer's fictionalised documentary of part of the same period, *The Armies of the Night*, with a poetic piece of journalism. Finally, as *Notebook*, the reader is invited to take the book on more than one level: the 'notebook' is that of both the journalist and the artist. The product of three prolific years for Lowell, and subject to a constant process of addition and revision (from June 1967 to June 1970), it consists of almost 300 'sonnets' (or as Lowell puts it, 'fourteen line unrhymed blank verse sections'[3]), which range from epigrams, epistles and anecdotes to poems which read like episodes from a long narrative poem or fragments from a verse autobiography, and from the unmistakably sonnet-like in voice and procedure, to poems which are merely hopped-up prose. In three related ways *Notebook* breaks new ground for Lowell: it attempts to get away from the air of completeness of the normal poetry book in favour of a kind of open-endedness, in which the book grows not laterally, but by agglomeration, with poems added to the middle in order to, in Lowell's words, 'fulflesh'[4] it; it works to a conception of poetry as 'total experience', with the poems offering up the poet's life for viewing as it is being lived; and it challenges the autonomy of the individual poem.

Contemporary politics provided a nervous edge to the panorama of civilisation presented in *Near the Ocean*, and back in the 'forties, the larger gestures; now it is something like a continuous warp to a woof of personal experience. In 'The Dyer's Hand', Auden suggested that, in our age, 'the mere making of a work of art is itself a political act,[5] and the poems of *Notebook* reflect the sense of artistic beleaguerment that prompted Auden's remark. But the process also works the other way. Politics is

2. At Lowell's public readings.
3. *N.*, p. 263.
4. *N.*, p. 264.
5. *The Dyer's Hand and other essays*, London (Faber) 1964, p. 88.

E

another gesture of 'the shaping spirit', an heroic confrontation by the imagination of the ephemera of contemporary life. In the second of two poems about the Pentagon March, Lowell writes:

> Where two or three were heaped together, or fifty,
> mostly white-haired, or bald, or women . . . sadly
> unfit to follow their dream, I sat in the sunset
> shade of their Bastille, the Pentagon,
> nursing leg- and arch-cramps, my cowardly,
> foolhardy heart; and heard, alas, more speeches,
> though the words took heart now to show how weak
> we were, and right.[6]

These lines point the ironies of the poet's new involvement in the political arena, how it arcs between the two extremes of sublimity and absurdity. Political man is, for Lowell, that same mixture of 'upward angel, downward fish' as the universal man of 'The Quaker Graveyard in Nantucket': the other March poem describes opposing soldiers as 'the Martian, the ape, the hero', and tells of how the marchers' 'amplified harangues for peace' met the state's exaggeratedly marmoreal monuments with a mixture of 'fear, glory, chaos, rout'. Though it is a familiar view of a 'Roman' civilisation that sees in contemporary America a mixture of stone and animal, grandiose and monstrous, law and lawlessness, in the conflict between the new radical Left and the Administration, Lowell's attitudes are also close to those of a liberal Russian writer like Turgenev when contemplating the struggle between young anarchy and mild Czarist oppression. Sadly, in America in the 'sixties, this position was an increasingly impossible one, in view of the patent inability of liberalism's 'plaintive, now arthritic optimism'[7] to solve the insolvable in Vietnam and in the ghettoes; and divided by a generation and his background from liberalism's successors, Lowell is somehow a casualty of its failure.

One familiar charge laid against the literary-liberal is that he sees only the human condition, the futility of personal involve-

6. *N.*, p. 54.
7. *N.*, p. 241.

ment, and the dubious possibilities for contemporary heroism; it is a charge Lowell's political poems in *Notebook* seem to court. Faced by a nation sharply divided between Left and Right, black and white, and young and old, he returns constantly to that other great moment of division in America's history, the Civil War, when a comparatively innocent heroism last had its fling. He refers to the Pentagon marchers as 'green Union Army recruits', and his 'Abraham Lincoln' is a comment on the contemporary dilemma of an idealist in a violent situation and under a very different kind of presidency from Lincoln's. Another poem about a Union martyr, 'Charles Russell Lowell: 1835–1864', opens with a description which suggests a lost aristocratic distinction about the heroism celebrated; but then our vision of the man alters to see him as a Hotspur:

> Charles had himself strapped to the saddle . . . bound to death,
> his cavalry that scorned the earth it trod on.[8]

The motives for heroism and public sacrifice have always been questioned and worried over by Lowell, whether in a Colonel Shaw, a Napoleon, or his earlier self in his 'fire-breathing Catholic C.O.' days, but never more so than in this book; his view of the hero is now characteristically deflating: 'the real hero might be someone who'd never get his pistol out of the holster and who'd be stumbling about and near-sighted and so forth'.[9] (Lowell, of course, is myopic.)

So, when he comes to the heroes of the young, Lowell not unnaturally sees a gap between rhetoric and experience, one that can so easily be filled with a sloganising violence:

> His voice, electric, was a low current whir;
> by now he'd bypassed sense and even eloquence;
> without listening, the audience understood;
> anticipating the sentence, they too stood
> for the predestined poignance of his murder,
> his Machiavellian Utopia of pure nerve.[10]

8. *N.*, p. 55.   9. *Alvarez*, p. 42.   10. *N.*, p. 185.

Another poem about a contemporary hero, 'Che Guevara', which appeared in a collection of poems about Che by various poets, has been described by Lowell as 'no more a tribute to Che than Shakespeare's Hotspur is a tribute'.[11]

> Week of Che Guevara, hunted, hurt,
> held prisoner one lost day, then gangstered down
> for gold, for justice—violence cracking on violence,
> rock on rock, the corpse of the last armed prophet
> laid out on a sink in a shed, revealed by flashlight—
> as the leaves light up, still green, this afternoon,
> and burn to frittered reds; as the oak, branch-lopped
> to go on living, swells with goiters like a fruit-tree,
> as the sides of the high white stone buildings over-
> shadow the poor, too new in the new world,
> Manhattan, where our clasped, illicit hands
> pulse, stop the bloodstream as if it hit rock. . . .
> Rest for the outlaw . . . kings once hid in oaks,
> with prices on their heads, and watched for game.[12]

This is a good example of how, in *Notebook*, Lowell seems to be constantly moving around, looking for a new focus; the details are handled kaleidoscopically. It is also an example of the way in which, at their best, these poems offer a beautiful balance between observed detail, personal comment, and larger significance, and of a poem which is both deeply meaningful in its own, autonomous right, and yet is enhanced by the poems following it in the sequence of which it is the opening poem— these include the two 'March' poems, and 'Charles Russell Lowell'. Like Colonel Shaw, Che had the power to choose life, and yet died; but this one man's death offers a myth of renewal, a revelation—however weakly and 'by flashlight'. Lowell shows a fine ability to fuse a contemporary situation, charted by a week's newspaper reports, to age-old religious and mythical dimensions of violence. The poverty of Che's death and its surroundings echo those of Christ's birth, and so Lowell is able to express

11. Note in *Viva Che! Contributions in Tribute to Ernesto 'Che' Guevara*, ed. Marianne Alexandre, London (Lorrimer) 1968, p. 75.

12. *N.*, p. 53.

his guilty feelings about both Che's death and its tragic, frittered waste, and about the universal poverty which prompted it. A photograph of a dead South American guerrilla leader thus answers the question that Lowell poses in another poem and which echoes throughout the book: 'Who can help us from our nothing to the all?'

For the Union Dead and *Near the Ocean* charted the ever-shifting, zigzag fashion in which the self and society meet: in many ways, the process here is simpler. Daughter and wife are the twin muses of *Notebook*, and the hero is the self-creating epic hero of Whitman:

> I stand face to face with lost ages—my breath
> is life, the rough, the smooth, the bright, the drear.[13]

More than any of Lowell's books, *Notebook* offers direct and intimate portraits of the poet himself, his wife and child, and his friends. In 1967, Lowell was fifty, and there is a sense of mid-journey about *Notebook*; the book ends with a sequence called 'Half a Century Gone'. Contemplating the passing of the years with a wry irony, he refers to himself as 'a lapsed R.C. caught mid-journey to atheist', and as a member of 'the going generation'; he announces: 'We're fifty and free', and then listens to his daughter, who says, 'the heartache, when we're fifty'. The book begins with a sequence of poems about Harriet; in *For the Union Dead*, Lowell told us that 'A father's no shield / for his child', and here there is a sense of shared vulnerability between father and child. The book ends with an 'Obit' to his wife:

> old wives;
> I could live such a too long time with mine.[14]

It is a book about domestic love, and in a deeply-moving Horatian way, of affection towards friends; some of the best poems are the verse epistles and miniature elegies and tributes to friends (Tate, Berryman, Eliot, Jarrell, Roethke, etc.) who have died, or represent a shared humanity. For all its nervous intelligence, it is a

13. *N.*, p. 245.
14. *N.*, p. 261.

very romantic book—warm and sensuous—and Lowell's aware-ness of the process of growth, time and ageing prompt a new delicate and tender lyricism, which stops just this side of senti-mentality:

> You rival the renewal of all seasons,
> clearing the puddles with your last-year books.[15]

Rebirth, new sources of energy: these are the themes of many poems in the book, such as the sombrely-beautiful 'King David Senex', and 'Seals', where in a more playful projection of the themes, Lowell reincarnates himself as a seal.

What can one say of the book as an experimental form? There are perhaps two ways of looking at *Notebook*: as an all-embracing, modern-style epic, and as a variation on the sonnet-sequence. With regard to the first, there is a kind of innocence in the face of reality of a kind similar to that which inspired another long American autobiographical poem, Whitman's 'Song of Myself', and the poetry of Whitman's successor, William Carlos Williams. Each poem 'eats from the abundance of reality', as Lowell puts it in his 'Afterthought'. Never before has Lowell captured so well the surfaces of life, and one is tempted to see *Notebook* as, in Lowell's words in the poem 'Stalin', 'an arabesque, imperfect and alive', or as a collage, mosaic, or collection of *objets trouvés*. Many of the poems are fragments, others lean heavily on their neighbours for significance. Lowell uses words such as 'intuitive', 'opportunist', 'impulse' and 'accident' in relation to the book's composition, and spontaneity and chance are used as creative principles:

> One wants words meat-hooked from the living steer,[16]

> Luck threw up the coin, and the plot swallowed,
> monster yawning for its mess of pottage.[17]

Here, Lowell is very near to the well-springs of modern experi-mental art; for example, in the book's constant cross-cutting of

---

15. *N.*, p. 92.   16. *N.*, p. 211.   17. *N.*, p. 255.

styles—telegraphic, surrealistic, naturalistic, lyrical, narrative, dramatic—there is something like the effect of a cut-up novel. With their sudden transitions, varying speeds, free associations, and kaleidoscopic effects, the poems reflect modern life, the way in which images focus on our consciousness. Lowell has obviously searched for, and to some extent found, a form equivalent in purpose to that of Pound's Cantos—a form for all occasions, and one that balances the order of art with the disorder of life.

Yet *Notebook* also has a quite old-fashioned lyricism about it. In spite of the poet's stated wish to avoid 'the themes and gigantism of the sonnet',[18] the book *is* a sonnet-sequence, with many sub-sequences, and draws upon most of the regular practices of the form. In the past, variations from the sonnet's regularity—normally only appreciable over the length of a sequence—have usually consisted of irregular numbers of lines, as in Meredith's 'Modern Love' sequence, or of added codas as in Hopkins, or of irregular rhyme-schemes. Lowell has stuck with rock-like fidelity to his fourteen lines, but abandoned rhyme totally as a working principle, as if he feels that the sonnet's mellifluousness and rhetoric largely stem from this. In its themes, the book is near to the conventional sonnet-sequence—Love, Death, Time, Friendship, Growth, Decay, the Life of Art, etc.— but the particular *frisson* one gets from reading it largely arises from the prose pull towards the fragmentary and open-ended, against the grain of the traditional sonnet's closed disciplines. If the poet has sacrificed the controlled stateliness of both the Petrarchan and the Shakespearean sonnets, he still relies heavily on the strong middle breaks of the former, and the strong openings and couplet endings of the latter.

The immediate literary inspiration behind *Notebook* seems to have been John Berryman's *Dream Songs*, which Lowell reviewed enthusiastically, and found 'one of the glories of the age'.[19] *Dream Songs* is a sequence of 385 poems—each of three 6-line stanzas, and with a persona called Henry—which, Berryman claimed, constituted one poem. In *Notebook*, the final sonnet before the book's series of codas is an important tribute to Berryman, which suggests an identity of purpose between the two poets

18. *N.*, p. 263.
19. In *The Harvard Advocate*, CIII, Spring 1969, p. 17.

('John, we used the language as if we made it.') and develops from two statements in Lowell's review of Berryman's book: 'he somehow remained deep in the mess of things' and 'with Berryman, each succeeding book is part of a single drive against the barriers of the commonplace'. Yet the titles of Lowell's and Berryman's books suggest important differences. Lowell rises above the 'mess of things' to a discursive, rational level, though there is a strong 'surrealist' element; Berryman works at a sub-conscious level where the collapsed syntax of the Songs reflects private and idiosyncratic concerns. In comparison with Berryman's, Lowell's language holds firm: it is a social, shared thing, suggests public roles, has roots in history, religion and literature. Berryman's alienation is much more explicitly the subject of his poems, and his derangement and mutilation of language relate much more directly to the daily pangs of the suffering artist, the victim baring his wounds, the isolate descanting on unbearable solitude. In one of the Songs, he writes:

> These songs are not meant to be understood, you understand.
> They are only meant to terrify and comfort.[20]

In *Notebook*, Lowell offers something less than terror, more than comfort.

The equivalent of Berryman's dream element is Lowell's 'surrealism'. In his 'Afterthought', Lowell talks of the importance for him of the 'bent generalization' and of 'words that seem right but only loosely in touch with reason'. Constantly in *Notebook*, there are two elements played off against each other: the shaping surface, with its uncompromising pattern of fourteen lines, its rational, objective observer, and its world of ideas and things; and the subconscious drama welling up, the experiencing sub-world. The 'surrealist' effect is also conveyed by the dislocated time-sequence, with the poems jogging backwards and forwards between past and present, as if the arbitrariness of time is part of the book's message. Ultimately, *Notebook* is another American obeisance to the here and now, the ever-repeating, ever-renewing present tense; but throughout the book, there is

20. *His Toy, His Dream, His Rest*, London (Faber) 1969, p. 298.

the time of the human and the non-human; of nature and of
art; of eternity and the temporal. There is a general sense of the
past's irredeemability—

> I am learning to live in history.
> What is history? What you cannot touch.[21]

> No moment comes back to hand, not twice, not once.[22]

—but we are all caught up in the flux of time. In the *Notebook*
world, the protagonist seems constantly trapped in a mesh of
present participles:

> Inching along the bayfront on the icepools,
> sea and shipping cut out by the banks of cars,
> and our relationship advancing or
> declining to private jokes, and chaff and lust. . . .[23]

In one poem, Lowell announces: 'Life by definition breeds on
change', and the book is full of the cycles and circles of history,
the generations, the seasons. Two seasons of change and growth,
spring and autumn, predominate; and the colour green is everywhere, the colour of birth and decay, and innocence:

> our green army staggered out on the miles-long green
> fields,
> met by the other army . . .
> his new-fangled rifle, his green new steel helmet.[24]

As Lowell says in his 'Afterthought', the 'plot rolls with the
seasons'; but though the reader might think this presages the
extraction of the last ounce of myth from the natural world, it is
worth remarking that there is more straightforward observation
of nature than in any of Lowell's previous books. So many of
the book's best images are from nature:

> they sun naked like earthworms on the puddly mall.[25]

21. *N.*, p. 103.   22. *N.*, p. 103.   23. *N.*, p. 80.
24. *N.*, p. 54.   25. *N.*, p. 179.

> the breath
> of the world risen like the ripe smoke of chestnuts.[26]

There is a particular magic in the way the natural images are made to relate to political matters: in one poem, for example, grass is 'dead since Kennedy'.

Notebook also conveys the sheer oppressiveness of civilised living, its loneliness and terrors, its isolation from the natural world:

> the horror of top-flight skyscraper villages
> is the stench of loneliness they give off—[27]

> Nothing more established, pure and lonely,
> than the early Sunday morning in New York—
> the sun on high burning, and most cars dead.[28]

But the natural processes constantly force an awareness of tragedy and death:

> Corruption serenades the wilting tissues.[29]

> skin lumping in my throat,
> I lie here, heavily breathing, the soul of New York.[30]

This is a book in which we are frequently reminded of both the 'horrifying mortmain of ephemera', and of individual tragedies. There is a very fine poem about the death of Michael Tate, son of the poet; in *Land of Unlikeness* and *Lord Weary's Castle*, there was the general suffering of innocent children, but now it is particularised. We also see death and tragedy on a world-scale, in such figures as Attila and Stalin, and in those who were victims of their own power—Robespierre, Charles V, Richard III and the Japanese Admiral Onishi:

> he chats in his garden, the sky is zigzags of fire.
> One butchery is left; his wife keeps nagging.
> Man and wife taste cup after cup of Scotch;

26. *N.*, p. 105.   27. *N.*, p. 246.   28. *N.*, p. 57.
29. *N.*, p. 249.   30. *N.*, p. 146.

how garrulously they talk about their grandchildren,
and when the knife goes home, it goes home wrong. . . .
For eighteen hours you died with your hand in hers.[31]

'When the knife goes home, it goes home wrong': how much
weight that simple sentence carries in the totality of Lowell's
work—there is a clear line between a poem like this and Lowell's
marriage poems, such as 'Man and Wife'.

In a book of this length, any reader will be able to find poems
to his liking. But does it offer anything more than a series of
moving, often brilliant perceptions about modern life as lived
by an extremely sensitive consciousness? In particular, what sort
of unity is there, and how meaningful is the sequence and placing
of poems? Is the only unity in the character of the poet himself?
Lowell disclaims that the book is 'a pile or sequence of related
material'[32] and yet, all the way through, groups of poems acquire
a living unity through their relatedness of tone and mood,
imagery, or theme and subject. For example, one group of poems
is related by the common theme of imprisonment, another by a
Charles River-blood analogy, and another one relates to 'Leaves';
there is a midwinter series about women. Poems frequently
acquire additional meanings by their placing; for example,
coming after the two 'March' poems as it does, 'Charles Russell
Lowell' is much more clearly a commentary on the universality
of a certain type of innocent heroism, than a simple tribute to
one of the poet's ancestors; the two 'Caracas' poems in the same
sequence, besides being about the South America that Che
Guevara fought to alter, relate the Caracas of El Presidente
Leoni to President Johnson's Washington. Yet Lowell has felt
free to alter the original sequences by additions, and the later
additions have tended to change the book's initial character by
introducing a more sombre tone, something considerably different
from the 'joys of living'.[33]

No doubt, future critics will argue over these additions as
heatedly as they now argue over Auden's revisions. Two things,
however, are worth bearing in mind: the book *is* a 'notebook',

31. *N.*, pp. 171–2.
32. *N.*, p. 262.
33. *N.*, p. 263.

a work-in-progress, and the later additions, with their darkly-pessimistic tone, do reflect the erosion of hope during the late 'sixties when an increasingly autocratic state power in America combined with a confused radical Left to numb liberal hopes of a peaceful settlement of the issues troubling American life. Secondly, the book's unity has to be created in the process of reading, and hence requires a particularly alert responsiveness. Something of the same is due to the book's many 'borrowings' —from Lowell's earlier books, from conversations, and letters, and in the form of 'imitations' of poems in other literatures. The total effect of these is to establish the sense that the demarcation line between art and life is constantly fluid. Some of the book's revisions are merely directed to helping the reader by making references more explicit; but other poems undergo such drastic surgery as to cast doubt on the wisdom of including poems that have achieved success elsewhere in a different format. What is one to make of the revision of 'Water', for example:

> The sea flaked the rock at our feet, kept lapping the
>   matchstick
> mazes of weirs where the fish for bait were trapped.
> You dreamed you were a mermaid clinging to a wharf-
>   pile,
> trying to pull off the barnacles with your hands.[34]

This *Notebook* version destroys the poem's fine balance of matter and form: the half-rhymes are submerged in the middle of lines, and the poem has lost its rock-like clarity of outline.

In writing *Notebook*, Lowell was caught up in some uncontrollable urge to create—and to re-create, and to de-create. In one poem he states:

> It's life in death to be typed, bound, delivered,
> lie on reserve like the old Boston *British Poets*,
> hanged for keeping meter[35]

and *Notebook* seems to be a sustained attempt to avoid this kind of deathly respectability. If in *Near the Ocean* Lowell talked of

34. *N.*, p. 234.   35. *N.*, p. 212.

getting energy from fading fire, here he has over-abundance of it, and swept away on a tide of creativity, he confesses 'My lines swell up and spank like the bow of a yacht', and talks of 'swimming in the sperm of gladness'. This Renaissance energy spills over into breathless one-sentence poems and a new playfulness; artfulness, whimsy and fancy have made a long-overdue comeback to the contemporary poetry scene. There is a delight in working the full gamut of languages. A visit to the dentist inspires this Feiffer-like vignette:

> When I say you *feel*, I mean you *don't*. This thing's
> metaphysical not sensitive:
> you come here in your state of hypertension. . . .
> You got brains, why do you smoke? I stopped smoking, drinking,
> not pussy . . . it's not vice. I drill here 8 to 5,
> make New York in the sunrise—I've got nerves.[36]

This is one of several poems which consist totally of speech: there is a new genius for speech in *Notebook*, wholly different from its occasional use in *Life Studies*.

Two contradictory forces are at work in *Notebook*: humility in the face of experience and a God-like desire to create one's own life: 'Common the clay, kingly the workmanship.' Many critics, particularly English ones, have deplored Lowell's assumption of sovereignty in this way: hence the titles of some reviews of the book—'The King as Commoner',[37] 'Snatching the Bays'.[38] Others have implied a basic dishonesty. Dannie Abse talks of the 'self-indulgence'[39] of *Notebook*, Donald Hall of its 'seedy grandiloquence . . . self-serving journalism',[40] and Ian Hamilton calls the whole enterprise 'shoddy', and charges Lowell with a 'pursuit . . . [and] expectation of . . . applause', and a surrender to 'self-parody, the strenuous but machine-like animation of dead mannerisms'.[41]

36. *N.*, p. 138.
37. John Bayley, *The Review*, 24, December 1970, pp. 3–7.
38. Douglas Dunn, *Encounter*, March 1971, pp. 65–71.
39. Dannie Abse, *The Review*, 29–30, Spring–Summer 1972, p. 4.
40. Donald Hall, *ibid.*, p. 40.
41. *A Poetry Chronicle*, London (Faber) 1973, pp. 107–10.

Still others have objected to the unfinished character of *Notebook*, the way it appears to offer the raw materials of experience and jottings in place of the finished product. Thus John Bayley sees 'a jungle of objects and moments', a 'mish-mash', 'a dazzle of limp dialogues', a 'voracious clutter of contingent hits and misses'.[42]

Admittedly there is much to justify this chorus of rejection. There are too many plangent, pathetic passages ('I beseech forgiveness from my wife and child'), a misfired Vergilian serenity, a tendency to send out too many big, bold signals for attention ('No destructive element emaciates / Columbia this Mayday afternoon'), where Lowell's Boston grandiloquence breaks through the demotic surface, and sometimes, a flip banality. Sometimes Lowell's frequent speculations, maxims, and aphorisms—

> We are all here for such a short time,
> we might as well be good to one another[43]

> Old age is all right, but it has no future[44]

—are not backed up with enough detail and specificity. In the above, the first has the air of a limp Frost epigram, the second, of a Dorothy Parker *bon mot*. Over an enterprise of this length, it is almost inevitable that form becomes mechanical, and the reader often feels that some poems have been pushed into a fourteen-line Procrustean bed, and others have been over-inflated to a length they can hardly bear.

And yet, finally, how wide the experience seems, how varied the responses compared to those of most recent poets, how alive and alert! Like Ted Hughes' *Crow* (another sequence) with its use of cartoon elements, *Notebook* is an expression of the way in which a poet of a consciously craftsmanly and disciplined kind pays tribute to the more unrestrained and immediate poetry of our time, and the demand for an instant, throwaway poem; a poet of the 'cooked' persuasion acknowledges the 'raw', to use

42. *The Review*, 24, December 1970, pp. 3–7.
43. *N.*, p. 136.
44. *N.*, p. 140.

Lowell's own terms[45]—though it is worth pointing out that there is much more of the 'cooked', highly-wrought type of poem than is apparent on first reading. Perhaps watching Lowell in the process of making his poems is a source of embarrassment for some, as though we are eavesdropping on an artist who has, until now, kept us at a safe distance; we have moved from art gallery to artist's studio.

In writing about Lowell's early poetry Hugh B. Staples said: 'Human success, normal love, conventional beauty, have no place in his vision of the modern world'[46], and Gabriel Pearson: 'The poems lack any vision of normal life from which to derive their ethics'.[47] This book makes up for the deficiency. But all these go with a sense of agonised conscience. The desire for involvement that brought about Lowell's participation in the Pentagon March has led to a book in which there is a minimal commitment of faith after the exposures of idealism in *For the Union Dead*, *The Old Glory* and *Near the Ocean*. But the book's surge of creative power, and its effort to make new, raise important issues. To what extent is it an irrevocable step? Is the randomness of the book's structure, curbed to some extent by a line of seasonal myth, the only one that Lowell can conceive of for his 'unrhymed sonnets'? As Lowell has treated his book as a 'manuscript',[48] to what extent does he see it as a launching-pad for future books?

In 1973 these questions were answered with the simultaneous publication of *History*, *For Lizzie and Harriet* and *The Dolphin*. A large number of the poems in the first two books had appeared in *Notebook*: only *The Dolphin* is entirely new. But all three books show Lowell making new orders out of the apparently lax forms of *Notebook*; as he says in the blurb to one of them, he hopes he has cleared the 'jumble or jungle' of *Notebook* and 'cut the waste marble from the figure'.[49] *History* and *For Lizzie and Harriet* group the old poems by subject; in *The Dolphin*, Lowell groups his poems by subject and a lightly-held myth of the creature of the

45. In Lowell's acceptance speech on receiving a National Book Award in 1960.

46. *Staples*, p. 14.

47. 'Robert Lowell', in *The Review*, 20, March 1969, p. 12.

48. *N.*, p. 264.

49. In the blurb to Lowell's *History*.

title. *History* is a large book which arranges *Notebook*'s poems on this subject chronologically, and adds another eighty or so poems. Its achievement in making history from pre-history to the present both continuous and contemporaneous is a consummation of one very strong element in Lowell's career. He has always had a sombre, cyclic view of history, one fostered by his reading of his favourite historians—North's Plutarch, Thucydides, Tacitus, Clarendon and Toynbee; it is history seen with something like Hawthorne's eyes: 'the disturbed eyes rise, / furtive, foiled, dissatisfied / from meditation on the true / and insignificant.' But how far Lowell has travelled philosophically in his constant journeyings through history! It is instructive to compare the present book's poem about a painting of Charles V by Titian with an early poem about the same subject, 'Charles V and the Peasant': the early poem was specifically about the 'night' of Protestantism and nationalism which saw the emperor off the map of history; the *History* poem is about the corruptions of power at all times. *For Lizzie and Harriet* and *The Dolphin* annotate the anguished breakdown of one marriage, and the possibilities offered by a new one, in a new context of England: Lowell has admitted their affinities with Meredith's sequence, 'Modern Love' ('the first marriage-torture, marriage-strife, poem'[50]).

In 'Why I write',[51] George Orwell suggested that a writer has four motives: sheer egoism; aesthetic enthusiasm; historical impulse; political purpose. Never in Lowell have these motives been so finely balanced as in his work from *Notebook* onwards. These liberated 'sonnets' are a responsive instrument for representing, sometimes decoding, the noises of modern consciousness; and perhaps in this Lowell's latest books are akin to 'The Waste Land' for its generation, a means to make flexible the muscles of contemporary poetry.

50. Quoted in Christopher Ricks, 'Profile: The Poet Robert Lowell—seen by Christopher Ricks', in *The Listener*, 21 June 1973, p. 831.
51. *Collected Essays*, London (Mercury Books) 1961, pp. 419–26.

8   One Life, One Writing

A generally unsympathetic critic of Lowell's poetry, A. L. French, has written: 'It is the distinction of Robert Lowell to have created a kind of poetry which is—or looks—immune to criticism.[1] This seems an extraordinary statement when one considers the sheer amount of criticism that greets each new book of Lowell's: of all living poets, he is surely the most written about, on both sides of the Atlantic? But French is touching on important issues. The critic of Lowell is often like the man in 'The Mouth of the Hudson': he has trouble with his balance, and tends to go to extremes of uncritical adulation or denigration. Moreover, there is a sense in which Lowell's poetry has the power to draw critics away from the words on the page and into other issues: the status of the poet in the contemporary world; the connection between public and private worlds in poetry; politics and psychology; the love/hate relationship of contemporary British and American poets. Then there is Lowell's tendency to outpace his critics; there is the variety of his work—drama, translation of various kinds, criticism, as well as the poetry— to contend with, and the way in which each new book of poems seems to cancel the dearly-won ground of its predecessor and stake out a new territory. It is this difficulty of getting Lowell's work into one simple focus which perhaps accounts for the tendency of Lowell critics to reach for a convenient abstraction— often of an apocalyptic kind; at various times, Lowell has been a poet of revolt,[2] of abdication,[3] of extremism,[4] of rebellion,[5] of

1. A. L. French, 'Robert Lowell: The Poetry of Abdication', in *Oxford Review*, IX, 1968, p. 5.
2. W. C. Jumper, 'Whom Seek Ye?: A Note on Robert Lowell's Poetry', reprinted in *Parkinson*, p. 62.
3. A. L. French, 'Robert Lowell: The Poetry of Abdication', in *Oxford Review*, IX, 1968, pp. 5–20.
4. A. Alvarez, *The Savage God*, London (Weidenfeld), 1971; New York (Random House), 1972.   5. *Staples.*

cancellation,[6] of extinction,[7] and (to spoil the sequence) of reconciliation.[8]

Altogether, there is a general feeling that, more than any other post-war poetry, the issues that Lowell's poetry raises are both extensive enough and important enough to justify the critic in feeling that the health, and even the existence, of contemporary poetry itself is involved. Gabriel Pearson has said: 'Lowell's whole enterprise has a significance far in excess of the aggregated meanings of particular poems or particular volumes.'[9] It is probably only in this sense that one can, or should, talk of an 'Age of Lowell',[10] for the kind of centrality that justifies talk of an 'Age of Yeats' and an 'Age of Eliot' has been lost. But like Yeats at the beginning of his career, Lowell had to assimilate the poetic orthodoxy of his time, and apply it in his own way and to a different scene. In 1960, Lowell wrote:

> Our modern American poetry has a snarl on its hands.
> Something earth-shaking was started about fifty years
> ago by the generation of Eliot, Frost and William
> Carlos Williams. We have had a run of poetry as
> inspired and sadly brief as that of Baudelaire and his
> successors, or that of the dying Roman Republic and
> early Empire. Two poetries are now competing, a
> cooked and a raw. The cooked, marvellously expert,
> often seems laboriously concocted to be tasted and
> digested by a graduate seminar. The raw, huge
> blood-dripping gobbets of unseasoned experience are
> dished up for midnight listeners. There is a poetry
> that can only be declaimed, a poetry of pedantry, and
> a poetry of scandal.[11]

6. John Bayley, 'Robert Lowell: The Poetry of Cancellation', in *London Magazine*, VI, June 1966.

7. *Ibid.*

8. David Bulwer Lutyens, 'Robert Lowell: Poet of Reconciliation', in *The Creative Encounter*, London (Secker & Warburg) 1960, pp. 128–200.

9. 'Robert Lowell', in *The Review*, 20, March 1969, p. 4.

10. Irvin Ehrenpreis, 'The Age of Lowell', in *American Poetry*, ed. I. Ehrenpreis, London (Arnold: Stratford Studies No. 7) 1965.

11. From Lowell's acceptance speech on receiving a National Book Award in 1960.

As earlier chapters of this book have indicated, the three American poets Lowell refers to above have had different roles to play in his development. Frost's poetry has always seemed too idiosyncratic for him to use in any immediate way; the assimilation of Williams was a long-term process. It was Eliot who was the immediate challenge at the outset of his career, though Lowell found in him a 'simplicity' and 1920's freedom that was hardly repeatable. In *Image and Experience*, Graham Hough challenges the view that Eliot has been a seminal influence on the poetry after him:

> Mr Eliot's version of English literary history is as much an orthodoxy as Matthew Arnold's was a generation before. Yet the direct effect on literary practice has been strangely small. There is no other poem of any significance remotely like 'The Waste Land'.[12]

But in Lowell's case, the influence is unmistakable; and it stems from a recognition that, though Eliot's position was a 'narrow' one, it was a unity:

> Eliot has done what he said Shakespeare had done: all his poems are one poem, a form of continuity that has grown and snowballed.[13]

Lowell's early career was an exploration and working-out of the contradictions in Eliot's work and achievement: his poetry was impersonal in intention, yet so very personal; there was the stress on tradition, yet it represented in itself the breakdown of tradition, and was associated with a modernism that was anti-traditional in bias; American, yet cosmopolitan; intellectual, yet colloquial. In his own poetry, Lowell has made a characteristic weave of the various strands that make up Tradition and the Individual Talent. At the outset of his career, in spite of his conversion to Roman Catholicism and his engagement with writers of the South, the art of the past was something less solid

12. *Image and Experience*, London (Duckworth) 1960, p. 7.
13. *P.R.*, p. 266.

than 'existing monuments form[ing] an ideal order';[14] in any case, statues and monuments have an ambiguous existence in Lowell's poetry, as symbols of the public world of values and order, objects undermined by lost social purposes, and images of petrifaction where the social role has hardened. Eliot's doctrine of Impersonality—'What happens is a continual surrender of himself as he is at the moment to something which is more valuable. The progress of an artist is a continual self-sacrifice, a continual extinction of personality'[15]—had to be revised to include an openness about personal and family matters. And it involved bringing Eliot back home, so to speak, to his origins, making the cosmopolitan poet available again for the American scene.

The particular difficulties involved in this ambitious venture were recognised early on by the reviewers of Lowell's first books. On the whole, he was well served by critics with whom he had personal or literary affinities—R. P. Blackmur, Allen Tate, Randall Jarrell. All three saw in the rebellious energies and forcing of the will in the early poetry unresolved tensions. Blackmur's review of *Land of Unlikeness*, in which he saw Lowell's Roman Catholicism as being at the centre of a clash between 'form' and 'sentiment', and pleaded for a 'tension of necessity' in which conflict would be accepted, has already been quoted.[16] Tate, in his Introduction to the same book, reflected that the 'symbolic language often has the effect of being *willed*', and pointed to an unsatisfactory relationship between the religious and the other elements in the book. His remarks imply that one way of resolving the dilemma could be by moving the poetry in the direction of the personal and the historical:

> . . . certain shorter poems, like 'A Suicidal Nightmare' and 'Death from Cancer', are richer in immediate experience than the explicitly religious poems; they are more dramatic, the references being personal and historical and the symbolism less willed and explicit.[17]

14. T. S. Eliot, 'Tradition and the Individual Talent', in *Selected Essays*, London (Faber) 1932, p. 15.

15. *Ibid.*, p. 17.

16. Chapter Two, pp. 26-7.

17. *London and Boyers*, pp. 1-2.

In reviewing *Lord Weary's Castle*, Randall Jarrell also saw a conflict; but in this case, it was a creative tension in a pattern of open and closed states:

> The poems understand the world as a sort of conflict of opposites. In this struggle one opposite is that cake of custom in which all of us lie embedded like lungfish —the stasis or inertia of the stubborn self, the obstinate persistence in evil that is damnation. Into this realm of necessity the poems push everything that is closed, turned inward, incestuous, that blinds or binds: the Old Law, imperialism, militarism, capitalism, Calvinism, Authority, the Father, the 'proper Bostonians', the rich who will 'do everything for the poor except get off their backs.' But struggling within this like leaven, falling to it like light, is everything that is free or open, that grows or is willing to change: here is the generosity or openness or willingness that is itself salvation; here is 'accessibility to experience'; this is the realm of freedom, of the Grace that has replaced the Law, of the perfect liberator whom the poet calls Christ.[18]

Jarrell is not only very perceptive about Lowell's 'forties poetry, but finely prophetic about Lowell's subsequent career. His characterisation of Lowell's poetry is just as applicable to the later work; for example, 'Waking Early Sunday Morning' not only takes as its theme this 'conflict of opposites' but embodies it in its structure, imagery and language, and 'Law' in *For the Union Dead* clearly echoes the phrasing of the Jarrell passage. Jarrell continues:

> Consequently the poems can have two possible movements or organisations: they can move from what is closed to what is open, or from what is open to what is closed.[19]

18. 'From the Kingdom of Necessity', reprinted in *London and Boyers*, pp. 19–20.

19. *Ibid.*, p. 20.

At the time Jarrell was writing, a critic could be forgiven for thinking that Lowell might resolve the contradictions and tensions of his poetry by moving in the direction of one or other of the current vices of American poetry; abstract, de-metaphored and directly metaphysical writing; sophisticated academicism; direct, unadorned experience. That Lowell did not, is partly a consequence of his recognition that 'A poem needs to include a man's contradictions. . . . In the writing of a poem all our compulsions and biases should get in, so that finally we don't know what we mean.'[20]

We have now come to recognise that such a monument of modern poetry as 'The Waste Land' includes its author's contradictions in a much nearer-the-surface way than Eliot's doctrine of Impersonality gave us warrant for, and to accept that many of Eliot's personal concerns in the poem related to extreme states of mental breakdown and sexuality. With Lowell, the compulsions and extreme states have been a surface matter right from the beginning; he has always been the poet of the trapped consciousness, caught in a struggle between suffering man, liberating artist and public conscience; and his work constantly acknowledges that the mass evils of society have their counterparts within us.

Because of this, the 'confessional' label as attached to Lowell soon merged with that of 'extremist'. The phrase 'extremist poetry' was used by A. Alvarez in articles and reviews in the 'sixties, and the subject was discussed at length in his book, *The Savage God*,[21] but a widely-influential article by A. R. Jones in

20. Stanley Kunitz, 'Telling the Time', in *Salmagundi*, I, iv, 1966–67, p. 22.

21. In *The Savage God*, pp. 12–13, Alvarez writes: '. . . he [the contemporary artist] is involved not simply in his emotions but in their sources, in his hidden motives and compulsions, in his own internal power politics and the roots of his own violence. His clinical awareness of all this has been created by his growing intimacy with psychoanalysis; so, too, has his cool, analytic attitude to his own distress. But he shares this cool with his audience; so the more ruthless he is with himself, the more unshockable the audience becomes. This pushes the artist into what I would call Extremism. He pursues his interests to the edge of breakdown and then beyond it, until mania, depression, paranoia and the hallucinations that come in psychosis or are induced by drugs become as urgent and commonplace as Beauty, Truth, Nature and the Soul were to the Romantics. . . . If all this sounds modish and self-indulgent. . . .'

It does: when one talks about the relation between an artist, his work, and

Critical Quarterly of Spring 1965, probably did more than anything else to establish the view that the 'poetry of extremism'
was the main line for poetry in our time, after the 'slightly faded,
though elegant, lucid, decorous and curiously irrelevant' poetry
that Jones sees as coming from English poets in the 1950's:

> However accomplished their poetry might be, their con-
> ception of man was severely diminished, the area of
> life, on which they established themselves so
> confidently, severely restricted. Those appalling
> images of mass horror that the war had released to
> communal consciousness—horror symbolised in words
> like Belsen and Hiroshima—hardly involved them, for
> the rational, ordered consciousness and traditional
> decencies could not contain or comprehend irrationality
> on this scale; the unloosing of the blood-dimmed tide,
> the anarchy that Yeats predicted, found poetry
> vaguely incredulous and totally unprepared.[22]

In this situation, Thomas Parkinson sees Lowell's value in that
he:

> dramatised, not knowing it himself any more than the
> rest of us, that pain was normal for our generation
> because of the irreconcilabilities we had chosen as our
> substance. . . . Pain was what we expected society to
> impose and all our cultural conditioning had led us to
> associate purgation and genuine suffering with that
> pain.[23]

Here is Alvarez:

> He (the artist) has to take the utterly psychopathic as
> his norm, and make art out of the forces of anti-art.[24]

---

his audience in this way, with a hectic style that preens itself on its indulgent
flail of assertions, one has moved into the realm of sensational journalism, or
of advertising and the big sell—whether applied to soap, or a poet.

22. A. R. Jones, 'Necessity and Freedom: The Poetry of Robert Lowell,
Sylvia Plath and Anne Sexton', in *Critical Quarterly*, VII, Spring 1965, p. 11.

23. *Parkinson*, pp. 143–4.

24. *The Savage God*, p. 26.

And Spender:

> Reading Berryman, Jarrell, Lowell, Roethke, and now
> this posthumous collection of Sylvia Plath, one is
> forced to take note that with some of the best recent
> poets, even though one does not immediately connect
> them with Rimbaud, a programme of the poet
> 'cultivating his hysteria' seems to have become very
> serious indeed.[25]

Now, one wouldn't wish to deny the very real perceptions
about Lowell that these and other critics of an 'extremist' persuasion have offered. But there is a danger of a new critical
orthodoxy taking root, which blankets over the very necessary
distinctions between 'dramatising' the harrowing experiences of
our century, 'cultivating one's hysteria', and 'making art out of
the forces of anti-art', and which does an injustice to the large
amount of good, 'unextremist' poetry being written in our time,
poetry which draws on a middle range of experiences, and is
often, without being provincial, rooted in particular native
traditions and works to shared conventions and languages.
Poetry such as that of R. S. Thomas and Seamus Heaney, like
that of Thomas Hardy and Edward Thomas earlier in the
century, still manages to convey and interpret the textures of
twentieth-century living: working at the edge of desperation is
not an infallible prescription for significance and relevance. Also,
there are very real differences between poets of the 'extremist'
group; the kind of distinction Ronald Hayman makes is an
essential part of recognising Lowell's importance:

> As with Sylvia Plath, the breakdowns, the poetry and
> the personal life are inextricable parts of the same
> whole but the drive towards sanity has been stronger,
> the awareness of the external world keener. His poetry
> is full of evidence of the depth of his concern about
> public and political events.[26]

25. Stephen Spender, 'Warnings from the Grave', in *The Art of Sylvia Plath*,
ed. Charles Newman, London (Faber) 1970, p. 200.
26. Ronald Hayman, 'The imaginative risk: Aspects of Robert Lowell', in
London Magazine, November 1970, p. 8.

The characterisation of Lowell as a poet of a personal 'extremist' art can only be partly true, for he always relates his inner turmoil to a context of extremism in America's past, in her present, and in the wider world.

In this century, but with a special acceleration since the war, there has been a movement from a view of art as consisting of the production of self-contained works to one of art as a heightened form of subjectivity, and this has led to our present uncertainties about impersonality. 'Confessional' and 'extremist' poetry are two post-war manifestations; beat and 'pop' poetry are others. Lowell has been a part of this movement, but in a complex and ambiguous way; the forces of tradition have always been stronger in his poetry than some critics have allowed for.

However, the view that Lowell's poetic output shows an overall sense of impersonal and objective coherence and relates to a traditional idea of the art-object has been challenged by several critics, including Robert Bly, A. L. French, Hayden Carruth, John Bayley and Thomas Parkinson. With different emphases, all are united in seeing Lowell as responding to the artistic currents of our time. Carruth writes:

> Lowell . . . is a poetic ego without fixtures: in a sense
> neither being nor becoming, but a sequence of
> fragments, like the individual frames of a movie film,
> propelled and unified by its own creative drive.[27]

Carruth goes part of the way with Lowell, and sees him as radically questioning fixed notions of art. Bayley, however, sees Lowell's poetry as 'a poetry of cancellation':

> Lowell's poetry looks out in an unexpected direction.
> It yearns towards non-existence. If a poetry can be
> said to have the death-wish, it has it. As his poetry
> has transformed itself it has perfected a capacity for
> self-extinction. The words of the early poems lie about
> helplessly, turgid and swollen; the words of the later

27. Hayden Carruth, 'A Meaning of Robert Lowell', in *Hudson Review*, XX, 1967, p. 445.

143

ones achieve a crispness of cancellation, leaving behind them only a kind of acrid exhaust smell.[28]

To Bayley, the poetry of alienation normally depends on a specially intimate relationship with the reader. But Lowell has broken traditional bonds for, in taking his alienation a stage further, the idea of an audience has gone:

> The writer alienated from society, the creator of madness, meaninglessness, the extreme situation—he is indeed a commonplace today, but the greater the alienation he describes the more uncomfortably close he comes to *us*, the reader, the more he depends on a personal relation with us. Like a drunk in a bar this author needs his finger in our buttonhole—the further off he is from the social and moral world the more urgent is his need to share his alienation with the reader. It is Lowell's achievement to have successfully alienated *the poem itself*, to have made it as unaware of us as the suicide caught by the camera flash. And this seems to me the real thing. It gives *Life Studies* and many of the later poems their quality of nicking the advanced edge of time, the moment that burns us before the unmeaning future and the numbed unordered past.[29]

Thomas Parkinson sees a danger in Lowell's confusing of the distinction between what a poem is *about*, and what a poem embodies and *is*:

> What happens in *For the Union Dead* is that so long as guilt and futility remain subjects, even attitudes, the poem can take care of itself; when they become the poem, the entire process breaks down. Then the poem is warranted by the momentum of the book, and since

28. John Bayley, 'Robert Lowell: The Poetry of Cancellation', in *London Magazine*, VI, June 1966, p. 77.

29. *Ibid.*, p. 78.

the linear movement has pace and direction, the book
doesn't suffer.

The poem does.[30]

Whatever the truth in these views—and many readers of
Lowell would probably want to balance them with an emphasis
on the pull of the conservative in his work—they do point to the
constant movement, change, and ambitiousness that has always
characterised his poetic career '(Somehow [I] never wrote
something to go back to'[31]). But these qualities have earned him a
great deal of suspicion and envy, particularly amongst English
critics and poets. Thus Douglas Dunn can say, 'I always sus-
pected someone had been appalled by Lowell's ambition',[32] and
in a symposium on 'poetry in the 'sixties' in *The Review*, Dannie
Abse suggested that the 'over-estimation' of Sylvia Plath and
Lowell was symptomatic of a desperate need to hail the arrival
of a new major poet.[33] In this same symposium, many of the
contributors expressed a general unease about the relation
between American and English poetry at the present moment;
according to one's choice, America's poets are now Big Brother
cultural imperialists, or English poets have retreated into a
cultural backwater to nurse their inferiorities. Alan Brownjohn,
in another issue of *The Review*, offered a useful summary of the
situation; he argued that English poetry has had a crisis of confidence thrust upon it by comparison with contemporary American
poetry:

> The principal symptoms of the neurosis wished on us
> are: a general lack of scale and ambition; a timid
> refusal to whip up some experimental vigour; a failure
> to seize chances, tackle the big themes, and face up to
> brute realities. English poetry, it is alleged, is at
> present altogether minor and unenterprising (though
> chapter-and-verse is not often given). English poets

30. *Parkinson*, p. 146.
31. *N.*, p. 213.
32. *Encounter*, October 1972, p. 43.
33. *The Review*, 29–30, Spring–Summer 1972, p. 4.

are worthy and honest in their own way, but sadly
polite and inoffensive. . . [34]

—and part of the trouble has been the shadow of Lowell's
evident stature. Brownjohn cited M. L. Rosenthal's 'Poetry of
the Main Chance' (an article in *The Times Literary Supplement*[35])
and A. Alvarez' famous 'gentility' article[36] as giving credence to
a false view of the qualities of contemporary English poetry. One
read his article with a warm sense that he was righting an
imbalance—English poetry has, after all, produced its classics
since the war; until one reached the end, and one's eye strayed
across the page to a poem by Molly Holden which began:

> Suburbia, like hanging, concentrates
> the mind most wonderfully, points here a view,
> a slice of sky . . .[37]

and predictably assured us that 'Delight's always available to
those / who need no burning-glass to urge the fire / of empathy':
perhaps the main characteristic of post-war English poetry *is*
its 'gentility', after all? Then one re-read Brownjohn's article
and found that, though he was rightly sceptical of the many
attempts at characterising contemporary English poetry, he
raised new aunt sallies in English poetry's 'native rationality
and scepticism'. And a recognition of why Lowell is important
seemed more urgent than ever.

One thing that perhaps led to a great deal of unease at Lowell's
position in the 'sixties was an increasing sense of the public voice
in his poetry, after he had apparently established himself as a
private and 'confessional' poet with *Life Studies*. In *The Truth of
Poetry*, Michael Hamburger argues that 'the distinction between
public and private poetry is valid if we apply it not so much to
subjects or themes as to the relationship between poet and reader

---

34. *The Review*, 24, December 1970, p. 41. This article is reprinted, in an
expanded form, in *British Poetry since 1960*, ed. Michael Schmidt and Grevel
Lindop, Oxford (Carcanet Press) 1972.
35. *The Times Literary Supplement*, 29 January, 1970.
36. Introduction to *The New Poetry*, London (Penguin) 1962.
37. *The Review*, 24, December 1970, p. 49.

posited by the very structure and texture of poems on any subject whatever.'[38] Lowell has written poems which are public by virtue of their subject or theme: the title-poem of *For the Union Dead* is an obvious example, but even here, one has to qualify the epithet 'public' by admitting that the poem is shot through with private concerns. But in Hamburger's second sense, Lowell's is probably the most public poetry of our time. The characteristic tone of a Lowell poem, and the relationship established with the reader, is one which assumes that the poem occupies a public realm to which both poet and reader have common access; the traditional public poem, however, is *about*, a 'statement' whereas a Lowell public poem *is*. In a valuable review of *Near the Ocean*, John Holloway characterised Lowell as a poet constantly striving towards a 'public dimension', though compromised at each stage:

> Lowell is a poet who, in most marked contrast to all his English contemporaries, has been willing and able to encompass the public and historical as well as the private and immediate. As a result, his work has a range and a vehement authority that—well, perhaps the best thing to do is simply call to mind Philip Larkin's 'Church-going', Donald Davie's 'Remembering the Thirties', Ted Hughes' 'Thought Fox' or Charles Tomlinson's 'Paring the Apple'. But, though that public-historical dimension may have been boldly his concern, Lowell has not encountered it with a single mind. There is an effort towards the public world, but (save, I think in a few passages of denunciation) there is no mastery of it or assurance within it.[39]

Holloway goes on to relate this to the communal character of nineteenth-century American poetry (as opposed to English), specifically, the poetry of New England:

> For long over a century, poetry in America, and literature indeed as a whole, has had a special relation

38. *The Truth of Poetry*, London (Penguin) 1972, p. 201.
39. 'Robert Lowell and the Public Dimension', in *Encounter*, April 1968, p. 76.

to nationhood and to the communal ways of life of a new state. Aside from obvious cases like Whitman and Melville (and Lowell's style and also his content clearly owe a great deal to *Moby Dick*), poems like Amy Lowell's 'Lilacs', Timrod's 'Ethnogenesis'— though this is not Federal but Confederate—James Russell Lowell's 'Ode' for the 1865, post-Bellum, Harvard Commemoration, or Whittier's 'Centennial Hymn', all testify along with much else to this dimension in 19th-century American poetry. New England was probably its most assured centre, and no one can overlook the recurrence, in the brief catalogue above, of Lowell's namesakes.

But in Lowell himself, assured acceptance of the communal *credo* has gone. What is left is the ambivalence of a tradition already on the way out. Admittedly, the American poets of the 19th century were not Vergils. The public status of the poet was even then dubious. But one thing is clear enough: the contrast with England.[40]

This is well put, though Holloway perhaps underestimates the extent to which the force of New England poetry had already gone into a different tradition—a poetry created out of the self; and there is perhaps an implicit under-valuation of the force of the 'public dimension' in the poetry of the South—particularly after the Civil War. Given the decline of the 'public dimension' in the literature of New England, there is a point in Lowell's early turning to the South for that sense of history, myth, moral authority which public poetry traditionally has, and one can see why Lowell could say wryly of the ambience of the 'Southern Renaissance': 'I realized that the dead weight of poor J. R. Lowell was now an asset. Here, like the battered Confederacy, he still lived and was history',[41] and why Ransom should predict that Lowell would become the Vergil of America

40. 'Robert Lowell and the Public Dimension', in *Encounter*, April 1968, pp. 78–9.
41. Robert Lowell, 'Visiting the Tates', in *Sewanee Review*, LXVII, October–December 1959, p. 557.

—though that role no one could fill, least of all, Lowell, whose work rarely suggests the serenity of Vergil.

How to achieve universality by marrying the richness of experienced personal life to communal themes: that has always been Lowell's problem. His sense of responsibility pushes him towards the social world, and his alienation never allows him to treat it with anything but anguish; but he has a strong conviction that outer and inner chaoses must be viewed as in a mirror, and that art has to be true both to experience and to a reality out there, and to be both criticism and creation. The complexity of the forces that go into the making of a poem has nowhere been better expressed than by Lowell himself:

> Almost the whole problem of writing poetry is to
> bring it back to what you really feel, and that takes
> an awful lot of maneuvering. You may feel the door-
> knob more strongly than some big personal event, and
> the doorknob will open into something that you can
> use as your own. A lot of poetry seems to me very
> good in the tradition but just doesn't move me very
> much because it doesn't have personal vibrance to it.
> I probably exaggerate the value of it, but it's precious
> to me. Some little image, some detail you've noticed—
> you're writing about a little country shop, just
> describing it, and your poem ends up with an
> existentialist account of your experience. But it's the
> shop that started it off. You didn't know why it
> meant a lot to you. Often images and often the sense
> of the beginning and end of a poem are all you have—
> some journey to be gone through between those things;
> you know that, but you don't know the details. And
> that's marvellous; then you feel the poem will come
> out. It's a terrible struggle, because what you really
> feel hasn't got the form, it's not what you can put
> down in a poem. And the poem you're equipped to
> write concerns nothing that you care very much about
> or have much to say on. Then the great moment
> comes when there's enough resolution of your technical
> equipment, your way of constructing things, and what

you can make a poem out of, to hit something you
really want to say. You may not know you have it to
say.[42]

The recognition that *Notebook* somehow crystallises the kind
of process outlined above informs Philip Cooper's book, *The
Autobiographical Myth of Robert Lowell*.[43] Cooper sees *Life Studies* as,
in a way, the starting-point of Lowell's career; the 'forties poetry
gets short shrift as, in the poetry of this period, Lowell had not
yet mastered the art of transforming autobiographical, secular
and prosaic materials into poetic myth, which is the main concern
of Cooper's book. Central to the book's argument is a sensitive
and touchstone reading of 'The Mouth of the Hudson', which
Cooper sees as both an exploration of the possibilities of colloquial
language and of the phenomenal world, and as a fine example of
myth-creation. For Cooper, Lowell's later technical preoccupations, and his concern with autobiographical material, represent
a progress from Symbolism back into life.

The rendering of personal materials into art in Lowell's poetry
is also traced in a very fine essay by Gabriel Pearson. Pearson
sees *For the Union Dead* as the 'nub' of the 'Lowell enterprise'
(how often this last word occurs in articles about Lowell!), for
in it, there is both an acknowledgement of the force of a non-
literary, vernacular tradition in American poetry—represented
by William Carlos Williams and Whitman, and with off-shoots
in Crane, Pound and the Projectivists—with its alternative to
the traditional view of poems as self-contained artifacts, and a
re-affirmation of 'the power of literature to order the chaos of
society, personality and history, with its own order, its own
virtue':

> Lowell projects a career, not a life: he is a professional,
> not, in a complex sense of the word, an amateur. The
> materials of his own life are there to be made over
> into art. Interest focusses on that process, not on the
> life itself as exemplary or holy. I intend only a crude

42. *P.R.*, pp. 268–9.
43. Philip Cooper, *The Autobiographical Myth of Robert Lowell*, Chapel Hill
(University of North Carolina) 1970.

distinction. Lowell does tie his poetry, sporadically, to the line of a biography. But the emphasis is towards self-sufficiency of poetic statement, and where this fails it registers as—except in *Life Studies*—a lack, an aspect of cultural deprivation which the poems take as their subject and seek to redress.[44]

Pearson backs up his arguments about the relation between art and experience in Lowell's poetry with several fine analyses of specific poems. Here is part of his account of 'Memories of West Street and Lepke':

> The poem remains an architecture that simulates, anticipates and thus prevents its own demolition. It is an artfully designed ruin. It only looks like a piece of nature formed haphazardly out of the forces of erosion and accumulation. Secular experience is never, ever, unmediated in Lowell. Not that, in verbal structures, it ever really could be, but, despite appearances, in Lowell's case the ultimate tendency of the poem is to insist upon its structure. Even in this poem, which comes nearer to unmediated existence than any other, in which the poem—the self-substantive, nominative thing—just manages to crystallise out of the stream of poetry—even here there is an appeal to a transcending notion of literature through which this poem takes its place with other poems as part of an order. We are in the presence of a Dejection Ode, of a literary *kind*, and it is that fact which resists the reader's own death-wish; it resists too any impulse he might have to drown and be absorbed in the poet's private substance which, until it is owned not as a wholly personal project but as a part of a joint human enterprise, must remain part of the chaos out of which order is still to be achieved.[45]

44. 'Robert Lowell', in *The Review*, 20, March 1969, p. 4.
45. *Ibid.*, pp. 35–6.

This view of the poem as an artfully-constructed 'Dejection Ode' contrasts markedly with Bayley's opinion that Lowell's poems are hell-bent on self-annihilation.

In 1945, Randall Jarrell predicted that Lowell might write the best poems of his age.[46] He has certainly written many of its finest; but what Jarrell probably couldn't have foreseen is the variety of the achievement, and yet the sense of a 'career' carved out at great cost. Behind it all has been an uncertainty. Lowell has never had the background sureties of Hardy and Yeats; the confidence of Pound; the staple of a 'tradition' of Eliot; or Stevens' calm, philosophic temperament. Sometimes in his writings and talk about poetry, Lowell has stressed craft; on other occasions, experience. But he has always been against *mere* craft, *mere* experience. Of Stanley Kunitz, he has written: 'He has never published an unfelt and unfinished poem', and of a Kunitz poem:[47]

> The reader feels the simple brute impact, but is ignorant of the sweat and science that carried the weight into position. In the working-out of a poem, I look for two things: a commanding, deadly effectiveness in the arrangement, and something that breathes and pauses and grunts and is rough and unpredictable to assure me that the journey is honest.[48]

The central line of American post-war poetry has emphasised the primacy of the poet's consciousness: hence the importance of Stevens' explorations of the relation between the imagination and reality. But with Lowell the imagination has been used with a new directness, and a moving beyond notions of the purity of the artistic process, and the consequence has been a new stress on the naked self, which owes a great deal to both Whitman and Emerson, and those explorers of the ambiguities and the darker side of the personality, Hawthorne and Melville.

And yet, Lowell has seen the dangers in erecting the artistic

46. In a review of *Land of Unlikeness*, 'Poetry in War and Peace', in *Partisan Review*, XII, 1945, pp. 120–6.

47. *Ostroff*, p. 75.

48. *Ibid.*, p. 74.

imagination as the highest good, or the only reality. He has said that 'a man is able to be an imagination and the imagination able to be disinterested and urbane only because it is supported by industrial slaves'.[49] Right from the beginning of his career, Lowell has been a poet who, moved by what he has seen as the lost promise of American civilisation, has brought his personal life to bear on the 'unforgivable landscape' of a country despoiled by centuries of capitalist and theological exploitation. He has shown himself to be a true representative of the liberal conscience in his opposition to what he considers repressive political and social policies, and nobody has captured so well in poetry the restrictions, the mind-sapping conformities, of living in a highly-developed Western society, and the basic animality of our civilisation at its worst. Yet, in pursuing the extreme edge of his life and of our society—in war, madness and violence—he encourages in us a gratitude that somehow our society can still engage the deepest insights of its poets:

> In all our affairs, your lines throb
> with the high charge of the world. Each wire is a
> conductor.[50]

49. 'Imagination and Reality', in *The Nation*, CLXIV, 5 April 1947, p. 400.
50. *I.*, p. 134.

Select Bibliography

Note: Where two or more editions of any work are listed, all references in the text are to the editions marked * in this bibliography.

1   Works by Robert Lowell

(i) Books

Land of Unlikeness, Cummington, Massachusetts (The Cummington Press) 1944, with an introduction by Allen Tate, and in an edition of 250 copies.

Lord Weary's Castle, New York (Harcourt, Brace) 1946; the second impression, 1947, has some revisions.

The Mills of the Kavanaughs, New York (Harcourt, Brace) 1951.

Life Studies, New York (Farrar, Straus & Cudahy) 1959 and 1967; London (Faber) 1959, but without '91 Revere Street'; New York (Vintage Books) 1960, a paperback edition, and also containing 'Colonel Shaw and the Massachusetts 54th'; London (Faber) 1968*, with '91 Revere Street'.

Imitations, New York (Farrar, Straus & Cudahy) 1961; London (Faber) 1962 and 1971*; New York (Noonday: Farrar, Straus & Cudahy) 1962, a paperback edition. See also *The Voyage* below.

Phaedra, first published in *The Classic Theatre*, ed. Eric Bentley, Vol. IV: Six French Plays, New York (Doubleday: Anchor Books) 1961. In *Phaedra and Figaro*, New York (Farrar, Straus & Cudahy) 1961; London (Faber) 1963 and 1971*.

For the Union Dead, New York (Farrar, Straus & Giroux) 1964; London (Faber) 1965*.

The Old Glory, New York (Farrar, Straus & Giroux) 1965, with an Introduction by Robert Brustein; New York (Noonday: Farrar, Straus & Giroux) 1966, a paperback edition; revised editions in 1968 and 1969; London (Faber) 1966*, with a Director's Note by Jonathan Miller.

Near the Ocean, New York (Farrar, Straus & Giroux) 1967 with illustrations by Sidney Nolan; London (Faber) 1967*.

The Voyage, Lowell's Baudelaire translations from *Imitations*, with illustrations by Sidney Nolan: London (Faber) 1968; New York (Farrar, Straus & Giroux) 1969.

Prometheus Bound, New York (Farrar, Straus & Giroux) 1969 and simultaneously in paperback; London (Faber) 1970*. First published in *New York Review of Books*, 13 July 1967.

Notebook, As *Notebook 1967–68*, New York (Farrar, Straus & Giroux) May 1969; second edition, with revisions, July 1969; revised and expanded edition, 1970; London (Faber) 1970*.

For Lizzie and Harriet, New York (Farrar, Straus & Giroux) 1973; London (Faber) 1973.

History, New York (Farrar, Straus & Giroux) 1973; London (Faber) 1973.

The Dolphin, New York (Farrar, Straus & Giroux) 1973; London (Faber) 1973.

The following volumes each combine two Lowell books:

Poems 1938–1949, London (Faber) 1950. This comprises the complete contents of *Lord Weary's Castle* and *The Mills of the Kavanaughs*, with the exception of the latter's title-poem.

Lord Weary's Castle and The Mills of the Kavanaughs, New York (Meridian Books) 1961, a paperback edition; New York (Harvest: Harcourt, Brace) 1968.

Life Studies and For the Union Dead, New York (Noonday: Farrar, Straus & Giroux) 1968, a paperback edition.

There are selections from Lowell's books in:

Selected Poems, London (Faber) 1965, a paperback edition.

The Achievement of Robert Lowell, Glenview, Illinois (Scott, Foresman) 1966, edited, with an introduction and notes, by William J. Martz.

Lowell's versions of poems by Anna Akhmatova and Osip

Mandelstam and Pasternak are in *Poets on Street Corners*, ed. Olga Carlisle, New York (Random House) 1968, the Mandelstam translations in *Atlantic Monthly*, CCXI, June 1963, pp. 63-8.

His Montale versions are in *Eugenio Montale: Selected Poems*, intro. by Glauco Cambon, Edinburgh (University Press) 1966.

(ii) Miscellaneous articles, reviews and criticism

'A Review of *Four Quartets*', in *Sewanee Review*, LI, Summer 1943, pp. 432–5.

'A Note' (on Hopkins), in *Kenyon Review*, VI, Autumn 1944, pp. 583–6.

'Imagination and Reality' (on Stevens), in *The Nation*, CLXIV, 5 April 1947, pp. 400–2.

'Thomas, Bishop and Williams', in *Sewanee Review*, LV, Summer 1947, pp. 493–503.

'Paterson 2', in *The Nation*, CLXVI, 19 June 1948, pp. 692–4.

'John Ransom's Conversation', in *Sewanee Review*, LVI, July–September 1948, pp. 374–7.

'Prose Genius in Verse' (on Robert Penn Warren), in *Kenyon Review*, XV, Autumn 1953, pp. 619–25.

'The Muses Won't Help Twice' (on A. E. Watts' translation of Ovid's *The Metamorphoses*), in *Kenyon Review*, XVII, Spring 1955, pp. 317–24.

'Visiting the Tates', in *Sewanee Review*, LXVII, Autumn 1959, pp. 557–9.

'I. A. Richards as Poet', in *Encounter*, XIV, February 1960, pp. 77–8.

'Yvor Winters, A Tribute', in *Poetry*, XCVIII, April 1961, pp. 40–3.

'William Carlos Williams', in *Hudson Review*, XIV, Winter 1961–62, pp. 530–6; reprinted in *William Carlos Williams: A Collection of Critical Essays*, ed. J. Hillis Miller, Englewood Cliffs (Prentice-Hall) 1966.

Contribution to 'The Cold War and the West' (a symposium), in *Partisan Review*, XXIX, Winter 1962, p. 47.

'On the Gettysburg Address', in *Lincoln and the Gettysburg Address*, ed. Allan Nevins, Urbana (University of Illinois) 1964, pp. 88–9.

'The Poetry of John Berryman', in *New York Review of Books*, II, 28 May 1964, pp. 3–4.

'On Stanley Kunitz's "Father and Son" ', in *The Contemporary Poet as Artist and Critic*, ed. Anthony Ostroff, Boston (Little, Brown) 1964, pp. 71–5.

'On "Skunk Hour" ', *ibid.*, pp. 107–10; reprinted in *Parkinson*, pp. 131–4.

Foreword to *Ariel* by Sylvia Plath, New York (Harper & Row) 1966. (Not included in English edition of *Ariel*.)

'Randall Jarrell 1914–1965: An Appreciation', in *The Lost World*, by Randall Jarrell, New York (Collier) 1966; reprinted, with a review of Jarrell's *The Seven-League Crutches*, in *Randall Jarrell: 1914–65*, ed. Robert Lowell, Peter Taylor and Robert Penn Warren, New York (Farrar, Straus & Giroux) 1967.

Contribution to 'What's happening to America', in *Partisan Review*, XXXIV, 1967, p. 38.

'Digressions from Larkin's 20th-Century Verse', in *Encounter*, May 1973, pp. 66–8.

2   Interviews with Lowell

ALVAREZ, A., 'Robert Lowell in Conversation', in *The Observer*, 21 July 1963, p. 19.

—— 'Robert Lowell in Conversation', in *The Review*, 8, August 1963, pp. 36–40. Parts of *The Observer* interview, plus new material, reprinted in *The Modern Poet*, pp. 188–93.

—— 'Talk with Robert Lowell', in *Encounter*, February 1965, pp. 39–43; reprinted in A. Alvarez, *Under Pressure*, London (Penguin) 1966.

BILLINGTON, MICHAEL, 'Mr. Lowell on T. S. Eliot and the Theatre', in *The Times*, 8 March 1967, p. 10.

BROOKS, CLEANTH & ROBERT PENN WARREN, *Conversations on the Craft of Poetry*, New York (Holt, Rinehart & Winston) 1961.

CARNE-ROSS, D. S., 'Conversation with Robert Lowell', in *Delos*, I, 1968, pp. 165–75.

GALE, JOHN, 'Keeping the lid on the world', in *The Observer*, 12 March 1967, p. 11.

GILMAN RICHARD, 'Life Offers No Neat Conclusions', in *New York Times*, 5 May 1968, Section 2, pp. 1, 5.

KUNITZ, STANLEY, 'Talk with Robert Lowell', in *New York Times Book Review*, 4 October 1964, pp. 34–8.

Life, LVIII (American edition) 'Applause for a Prize Poet', 19 February 1965, pp. 49–58.

McCORMICK, JOHN, 'Falling Asleep over Grillparzer: An Interview with Robert Lowell', in *Poetry*, LXXXI, January 1953, pp. 269–79.

NAIPAUL, V. S., 'Et in American Ego—the American poet Robert Lowell talks to the novelist V. S. Naipaul, etc.', in *The Listener*, 4 September 1969, pp. 302–4; A Conversation with Robert Lowell, *The Review*, 26, Summer 1971, pp. 10–29.

SEIDEL, FREDERICK, 'Interview with Robert Lowell', in *Paris Review*, VII, Winter–Spring 1961, pp. 56–95. Reprinted in *Writers at Work: The Paris Review Interviews, Second Series*, New York (Viking Press) 1963, pp. 335–68, and London (Secker & Warburg) 1963. Also, in *Modern Poets on Modern Poetry*, ed. James Scully*, London (Collins: Fontana) 1966, pp. 237–69; in *London and Boyers*, pp. 261–91; in *Parkinson*, pp. 12–35.

3 Criticism of Lowell

(i) Books on Lowell

COOPER, PHILIP, *The Autobiographical Myth of Robert Lowell*, Chapel Hill (University of North Carolina) 1970.

COSGRAVE, PATRICK, *The Public Poetry of Robert Lowell*, London (Gollancz) 1970.

FEIN, RICHARD J., *Robert Lowell*, in Twayne's United States Authors Series, New York (Twayne Publishers, Inc.) 1970.

LONDON, MICHAEL & ROBERT BOYERS (eds.), *Robert Lowell: A Portrait of the Artist in his Time*, New York (David Lewis) 1970.

MARTIN, JAY, *Robert Lowell*, in University of Minnesota Pamphlets on American Writers series, Minneapolis (University of Minnesota Press) 1970.

MAZZARO, JEROME, *The Poetic Themes of Robert Lowell*, Ann Arbor (University of Michigan) 1965.

MEINERS, R. K., *Everything to be endured: an essay on Robert Lowell and modern poetry, etc.* Columbia (University of Missouri Press) 1970.

PARKINSON, THOMAS (ed.), *Robert Lowell: A Collection of Critical Essays*, Englewood Cliffs (Prentice-Hall) 1968.

PRICE, JONATHAN (ed.), *Critics on Robert Lowell*, Coral Gables, Florida (University of Miami) 1972.

STAPLES, HUGH B., *Robert Lowell: The First Twenty Years*, New York (Farrar, Straus & Cudahy) 1962; London (Faber) 1962*.

Magazines which have had special issues devoted to Lowell include: *Harvard Advocate*, LXLV, November 1961; *The Hollins Critic*, IV, February 1967; *Salmagundi*, Vol. I, No. 4, 1966–67.

(ii) Some general studies with chapters or pages devoted to Lowell

ALVAREZ, A., *Beyond All This Fiddle*, London (Allen Lane) 1968.

—— *The Savage God*, London (Weidenfeld & Nicholson) 1971.

BEWLEY, MARIUS, *The Complex Fate*, London (Chatto) 1952.

BLACKMUR, R. P., *Form and Value in Modern Poetry*, New York (Doubleday: Anchor) 1952.

—— *Language as Gesture*, London (Allen & Unwin) 1954.

CAMBON, GLAUCO, *The Inclusive Flame: Studies in American Poetry*, Bloomington (Indiana University) 1963.

DODSWORTH, MARTIN, *The Survival of Poetry*, London (Faber) 1970.

DONOGHUE, DENIS, *Connoisseurs of Chaos: Ideas of Order in Modern American Poetry*, New York (Macmillan) 1965; London (Faber) 1966.

EDWARDS, THOMAS R., *Imagination and Power: A Study of Poetry on Public Themes*, London (Chatto) 1971.

EHRENPREIS, IRVIN (ed.), *American Poetry*, (Stratford Studies No. 7), London, (Arnold) 1965.

GROSS, HARVEY, *Sound and Form in Modern Poetry*, Ann Arbor (University of Michigan) 1964.

HAMILTON, IAN (ed.), *The Modern Poet*, London (Macdonald) 1968; New York (Horizon Press) 1969.

—— *A Poetry Chronicle*, London (Faber) 1973.

HUNGERFORD, E. B. (ed.), *Poets in Progress*, Evanston (Northwestern) 1962.

HUSSEY, M., *Criticism in Action*, London (Longmans) 1970.

JARRELL, RANDALL, *Poetry and the Age*, New York (Knopf) 1953, and (Vintage Books) 1955; London (Faber) 1955.

LUTYENS, DAVID BULWER, *The Creative Encounter*, London (Secker & Warburg) 1960.

MAILER, NORMAN, *The Armies of the Night*, Cleveland (The World Publishing Co.), New York (New American Library) 1968; London (Weidenfeld & Nicholson; Penguin) 1968.

MILLS, JR., RALPH J., *Contemporary American Poetry*, New York (Random House) 1965.

OSTROFF, ANTHONY (*ed.*), *The Contemporary Poet as Artist and Critic*, New York (Little, Brown) 1964.

RABAN, JONATHAN, *The Society of the Poem*, London (Harrap) 1971.

ROSENTHAL, M. L. *The Modern Poets: A Critical Introduction*, New York (O.U.P.) 1960.

—— *The New Poets*, New York (O.U.P.) 1967.

SPEARS, MONROE K., *Dionysius and the City*, New York (O.U.P.) 1970.

STEINER, GEORGE, *Language and Silence*, New York (Atheneum) 1967; London (Faber) 1967.

STEPANCHEV, STEPHEN, *American Poetry Since 1945*, New York (Harper & Row) 1965.

(iii) Articles and reviews on Lowell

The 'Lowell industry' in colleges and universities is rapidly approaching the proportions of those devoted to Yeats, Pound and Eliot. In these circumstances, the following list can only claim to be a selection of some of the more interesting and influential (and on the whole, more accessible) of the many articles on Lowell.

ALVAREZ, A., 'A change in the weather' (on *Notebook*), in *The Observer*, 8 November 1970, p. 31.

ARROWSMITH, WILLIAM, 'Five Poets', in *Hudson Review*, IV, 1951-

1952, pp. 619–27; part reprinted in *London and Boyers*, and in *Parkinson*.

AXELROD, STEVEN, 'Baudelaire and the Poetry of Robert Lowell', in *Twentieth Century Literature*, XVII, 1971, pp. 257–74.

BAGG, ROBERT, 'The Rise of Lady Lazarus' (Yeats, Lowell, Eliot, Plath and the 'self'), in *Mosaic*, 2, iv, 1969, pp. 9–36.

BAYLEY, JOHN, 'Robert Lowell: The Poetry of Cancellation', in *London Magazine*, VI, June 1966, pp. 76–85, reprinted in *London and Boyers*.

—— 'The King as Commoner', *in The Review*, 24, December 1970, pp. 3–7.

BELITT, BEN, '*Imitations*: Translation as Personal Mode', in *Salmagundi*, I, iv, 1966–67, pp. 44–56; reprinted in *London and Boyers*.

BENNETT, JOSEPH, 'Two Americans, a Brahmin and the Bourgeoisie', in *Hudson Review*, XII, Autumn 1959, pp. 431–9; reprinted in *London and Boyers*.

BERRYMAN, JOHN, 'Lowell, Thomas, etc.', in *Partisan Review*, XIV, 1947, pp. 73–85.

—— 'On "Skunk Hour" ', in *Ostroff*; reprinted in *Parkinson*.

BLACKMUR, R. P., 'Notes on Eleven Poets', in *Kenyon Review*, VII, 1945, pp. 339–52; reprinted in *Language as Gesture*, London (Allen & Unwin) 1954, pp. 352–63. Also, in *London and Boyers*, and in *Parkinson*.

BLY, ROBERT, 'Robert Lowell's *For the Union Dead*', in *Sixties*, VIII, 1966, pp. 93–6; reprinted in *London and Boyers*.

BOWEN, ROGER, 'Confession and Equilibrium: Robert Lowell's poetic development', in *Criticism*, XI, 1969, pp. 78–93.

BRUSTEIN, ROBERT, Introduction to *The Old Glory*; reprinted in *Price*, 1965.

—— 'We Are Two Cultural Nations', in *New Republic*, CLI, 21 November 1964, pp. 25–30; reprinted in *Seasons of Discontent*, New York, London (Cape) 1966, pp. 252–9; and in *London and Boyers*.

CALHOUN, R. J., 'Lowell's "My Last Afternoon with Uncle Devereux Winslow" ', in *The Explicator*, XXIII, January 1965, pp. 40–3.

CAMBON, GLAUCO, ' "Dea Roma" and Robert Lowell', in *Accent*, XX, 1960, pp. 51–61.

CARNE-ROSS, DONALD, 'The Two Voices of Translation', in *Parkinson*, pp. 152–70.

CARRUTH, HAYDEN, 'A Meaning of Robert Lowell', in *Hudson Review*, XX, 1967, pp. 429–47; reprinted in *London and Boyers*.

CHADWICK, C., 'Meaning and Tone', in *Essays in Criticism*, XIII, 1963, pp. 432–5; reprinted in *Price*.

DANIELS, MAY, 'A Matter of Translation', in *Critical Survey*, V, No. 3, 1971, pp. 234–8.

DEWHURST, KEITH, On *Notebook*, in *The Guardian*, 6 January, 1971, p. 8.

DOHERTY, PAUL C., 'The Poet as Historian', in *Concerning Poetry*, Fall 1968, pp. 37–41.

DOLAN, PAUL J., 'Lowell's "Quaker Graveyard": Poem & Tradition', in *Renascence*, 21, 1969, pp. 171–80, 194.

DUNN, DOUGLAS, Review of *Notebook*, in *Encounter*, March 1971, pp. 65–71.

EBERHART, RICHARD, 'Four Poets', in *Sewanee Review*, LV, 1947, pp. 324–36; reprinted in *Parkinson*.

—— 'Five Poets', in *Kenyon Review*, XIV, 1952, pp. 168–76; reprinted in *London and Boyers*.

EULERT, DONALD, 'Robert Lowell and William Carlos Williams', in *English Language Notes*, V, December 1967, pp. 129–35.

FEIN, RICHARD J., 'The Trying-Out of Robert Lowell', in *Sewanee Review*, LXXII, 1964, pp. 131–9.

—— 'Mary and Bellona: The War Poetry of Robert Lowell', in *Southern Review*, I, 1965, pp. 820–34.

FRENCH, A. L., 'Robert Lowell: The Poetry of Abdication', in *Oxford Review*, IX, 1968, pp. 5–20.

FRIED, MICHAEL, 'The Achievement of Robert Lowell', in *London Magazine*, October 1967, pp. 54–64.

GRAY-LEWIS, S. W., 'Too late for Eden—An Examination of Some Dualisms in *The Mills of the Kavanaughs*', in *Cithara*, V, May 1966, pp. 41–51.

HAMILTON, IAN, 'Robert Lowell', in *The Review*, 3, August–September 1962; reprinted in *The Modern Poet*.

HARTMAN, G., 'The Eye of the Storm', in *Partisan Review*, XXXII, Spring 1965, pp. 277–80; reprinted in *London and Boyers*.

HAYMAN, RONALD, 'The imaginative risk: Aspects of Robert Lowell', in *London Magazine*, November 1970, pp. 8–30.

HELMICK, E. T., 'The Civil War Odes of Lowell and Tate', in *Georgia Review*, XXV, 1971, pp. 51–5.

HILL, G., 'Robert Lowell: "Contrasts and Repetitions"', in *Essays in Criticism*, XIII, 1963, pp. 188–97; reprinted in *Price*.

HOCHMANN, B., 'Robert Lowell's "The Old Glory"', in *Tulane Drama Review*, XI, Summer 1967, pp. 127–38.

HOFFMAN, D., 'Robert Lowell's *Near the Ocean*: The Greatness and Horror of Empire', in *The Hollins Critic*, IV, 4 February 1967, pp. 1–16.

HOLDER, ALAN, 'The Flintlocks of the Fathers: Robert Lowell's Treatment of the American Past', in *New England Quarterly*, 44, 1971, pp. 40–65.

HOLLANDER, JOHN, 'Robert Lowell's New Book', in *Poetry*, XCV, 1959, pp. 41–6; reprinted in *Price*.

HOLLOWAY, JOHN, 'Robert Lowell and the Public Dimension', in *Encounter*, April 1968, pp. 73–9.

HOWARD, RICHARD, 'Fuel on the Fire', in *Poetry*, CX, 1967, pp. 413–5; reprinted in *London and Boyers*.

ILSON, ROBERT, ' "Benito Cereno" from Melville to Lowell', in *Salmagundi*, I, iv, 1966–67, pp. 78–86; reprinted in *Parkinson*.

JARRELL, RANDALL, 'From the Kingdom of Necessity', in *The Nation*, CLXIV, 1947, pp. 74–7; reprinted in *Poetry and the Age, London and Boyers, Parkinson*, and *Price*.

—— 'A View of Three Poets', in *Partisan Review*, XVIII, 1951, pp. 691–700; reprinted in *Poetry and the Age, London and Boyers*, and *Parkinson*.

JONES, A. R., 'Necessity and Freedom: The Poetry of Robert Lowell, Sylvia Plath, and Anne Sexton', in *Critical Quarterly*, VII, Spring 1965, pp. 11–30.

JUMPER, W. C., 'Whom Seek Ye?' in *Hudson Review*, IX, 1956, pp. 117–25; reprinted in *Parkinson*.

LEIBOWITZ, HERBERT, 'Robert Lowell: Ancestral Voices', in *Salmagundi*, I, iv, 1966–67, pp. 25–43; reprinted in *London and Boyers*.

LINK, HILDA, 'A Tempered Triumph', in *Prairie Schooner*, XLI, 1967–68, pp. 439–42.

McCALL, DAN, 'Robert Lowell's "Hawthorne" ', in *New England Quarterly*, XXXIX, 1966, pp. 237–9.

MAHON, DEREK, Review of *Near the Ocean*, in *Phoenix*, 2, Summer 1967, pp. 50–4.

MARTIN, GRAHAM, 'Wastelanders', in *The Listener*, LXXVIII, 1967, pp. 311–2.

MARTZ, LOUIS, Reviews of *Notebook*, in *Yale Review*, LIX, 1969, and LX, 1970. The first is reprinted in *Price*.

MAZZARO, JEROME, 'Robert Lowell and the Kavanaugh Collapse', in *University of Windsor Review*, V, Autumn 1969, pp. 1–24.

—— On *The Old Glory*, in *Western Humanities Review*, 24, Autumn 1970, pp. 347–58.

MEREDITH, WILLIAM, on *Notebook*, in *New York Times Book Review*, 15 June 1969, pp. 1, 27; reprinted in *Price*.

MOLE, JOHN, 'Robert Lowell' (a poem), in *The Love Horse*, Manchester (Peterloo Poets series: E. J. Morten) 1973, p. 29.

MOON, SAM, 'Master as Servant', in *Poetry*, CVIII, 1966, pp. 189–90.

NELSON, R. L., 'A Note on the Evolution of Robert Lowell's "The Public Garden" ', in *American Literature*, XLI, 1969, pp. 106–110.

NIMS, J. F., 'Two Catholic Poets', in *Poetry*, LXV, 1944–45, pp. 264–8.

NITCHIE, G. W., 'The Importance of Robert Lowell', in *Southern Review*, Winter 1972.

PARKINSON, THOMAS, '*For the Union Dead*', in *Salmagundi*, I, iv, 1966–67, pp. 87–95; reprinted in *Parkinson*.

PEARSON, GABRIEL, 'Robert Lowell', in *The Review*, 20, March 1969, pp. 3–36, reprinted as 'Lowell's Marble Meanings', in *The Survival of Poetry*, pp. 56–99.

—— Review of *For Lizzie and Harriet*, *History* and *The Dolphin*, in *The Guardian*, 21 June 1973, p. 14.

PERLOFF, MARJORIE, 'Realism and the Confessional Mode of Robert Lowell', in *Contemporary Literature*, 11, 1970, pp. 470–87.

—— 'Death by Water: The Winslow Elegies of Robert Lowell', in *English Literary History*, XXXIV, 1967, pp. 116–40.

POIRIER, RICHARD, 'Our Truest Historian', in *Book Week*, 2, 11 October 1964, pp. 1, 16; reprinted in *Price*.

POWELL, G. E., 'Robert Lowell and Theodore Roethke: Two Kinds of Knowing', in *Southern Review*, January 1967, pp. 180–5.

PRICE, JONATHAN, 'Fire against Fire', in *Works*, I, Autumn 1967, pp. 120–6; reprinted in *Price*.

RAIZIS, M. B., 'Robert Lowell's *Prometheus Bound*', in *Studies in American Literature in Honour of Robert Duncan Faner*, ed. Robert Partlow, 1969, pp. 154–68: *Papers on Language and Literature*, 5, Supp.

RICKS, C., 'The Three Lives of Robert Lowell', in *New Statesman*, 26 March 1965, pp. 496–7.

—— 'Profile: The Poet Robert Lowell', in *The Listener*, 21 June 1973, pp. 830–2.

ROSENTHAL, M. L., 'Poetry as Confession', in *The Nation*, CXC, 1959, pp. 154–5; reprinted in *Price*.

SIMON, JOHN, 'Abuse of Privilege: Lowell as Translator', in *Hudson Review*, XX, 1967–68, pp. 543–62; reprinted in *London and Boyers*.

—— 'Strange Devices on the Banner', in *New York Herald Tribune Book Review*, 20 February 1966, pp. 4, 20; reprinted in *London and Boyers*, and *Price*.

SIMPSON, LOUIS, 'Matters of Tact', in *Hudson Review*, XIV, 1961–1962, pp. 614–7; reprinted in *London and Boyers*.

SNODGRASS, W. D., 'In Praise of Robert Lowell', in *The New York Review of Books*, 3 December 1964, p. 8, 10.

SOLOMON, SAMUEL, 'Racine and Lowell', in *London Magazine*, October 1966, pp. 29–42.

SPACKS, P. M., 'From Satire to Description', in *Yale Review*, LVIII, 1969, pp. 232–48.

STANDERWICK, DESALES, 'Pieces too Personal', in *Renascence*, XIII, 1960, pp. 53–6; reprinted in *Price*.

STEINER, GEORGE, 'Two Translations', in *Kenyon Review*, XXIII, 1961, pp. 714–21.

TATE, ALLEN, Introduction to *Land of Unlikeness*; reprinted in *London and Boyers*, *Parkinson*, and *Price*.

TOYNBEE, PHILIP, Review of *Near the Ocean*, in *The Observer*, 2 July 1967, p. 20.

WAIN, JOHN, 'The New Robert Lowell', in *New Republic*, CLI, 17 October 1964, pp. 21–3; reprinted in *London and Boyers*.

WEALES, GERALD, 'Robert Lowell as Dramatist', in *Shenandoah*, XX, Autumn 1968, pp. 3–28.

WIEBE, D. E., 'Mr Lowell and Mr Edwards', in *Contemporary Literature*, III, 1962, pp. 21–31.

WILBUR, RICHARD, On 'Skunk Hour', in *Ostroff*.

WILLIAMS, WILLIAM CARLOS, 'In a Mood of Tragedy', in *New York Times Book Review*, 22 April 1951, p. 6; reprinted in *Parkinson* and *Price*.

WOODSON, THOMAS, 'Robert Lowell's "Hawthorne": Yvor Winters and the American Literary Tradition', in *American Quarterly*, XIX, 1967, pp. 575–82.

4　Bibliographies

LONDON, MICHAEL AND BOYERS, ROBERT, In *Robert Lowell: A Portrait of the Artist in His Time*, 'A Checklist: 1939–1968', prepared by Jerome Mazzaro.

MAZZARO, JEROME, *The Achievement of Robert Lowell: 1939–1959*.

STAPLES, HUGH B., As an Appendix to *Robert Lowell: The First Twenty Years*.